# Politically Incorrect Ramblings

L.A. Stoner

*Politically Incorrect Ramblings*

Published by Hudson Books



Printed in the United States of America

*Politically Incorrect Ramblings*
L.A. Stoner

1. Title 2. Author 3. Humor/Essay

Library of Congress Control Number: 2009934931

ISBN 10: 0-9822553-1-4
ISBN 13: 978-0-9822553-1-5

*This book is dedicated to my amazingly supportive children and equally amazing significant other.*

*"Life is a long and beautiful journey. The joy is not in getting to the end of the road unscathed, but in the speed bumps, flat tires, and messy road conditions along the way."*

## Contents

## Book Four: Common Sense



## Book Five: Completely Pointless Rambling

# Foreword

This is a collection of personal observations; not facts. Three people are watching a sunset: the first comments on how pretty the pink sunset is, the second comments on how beautiful the purple hues are, and the third person comments on how the brightness hurts her eyes, which is not enjoyable. The three people are observing the same sunset, but each has their own personal observations. Who is right? No one and everyone. Are my observations right or wrong? Neither. Find your open-mindedness and sense of humor.

*"As I sit, head in hand gazing out at the night,*
*I see myself skitter by.*
*I am a single, solitary leaf blowing past on the crust of the barren, snow-covered landscape.*
*Direction and purpose seem hidden and mysterious.*
*Fickle fate blows strong, pushing me along."*
*—L.A. Stoner*

*"Whenever two people argue over principles,*
*they are both right."*
*—Marie Ebner Von Eschenbach*

# Book One:
# Spirituality

# Spiritual Business

I am a very spiritual person. I hesitate to call myself religious. I have spent a lifetime honing my spiritual comfort zone. I step closer to things that make me feel comfortable and peaceful and I step further away from the situations and people that make me feel nervous, afraid, and uncomfortable. I find that I feel the most at peace when I am alone in nature. I've always enjoyed a good sermon. I could usually find something for my brain to ponder that felt applicable to me and my life. My theory on being a good person, a "religious" person is simple: treat people, animals, and the planet the way you want to be treated. If you stop and listen to your conscience, it will tell you if what you are doing is right. When you have a quandary or are not sure what to do about a particular situation, sit quietly and ask your question. If you clear your mind and listen carefully the answer is already reverberating around in your conscience; It was already there before you asked the question.

I know people who continue to make choices that are selfish and self-centered. They wonder why they need drugs and alcohol or other addictions to feel good. I believe that God, or whatever term makes you most comfortable, resides in each and every one of us. We just need to listen. We know right from wrong, but just do not listen to that little, inner voice that is trying to guide us.

During early childhood I went to church because that is what my family said I had to do. I colored in all the e's and o's in my church bulletin to pass the time during the never-ending church service. I lip-synced the words to the songs as they didn't have much meaning for me yet and I couldn't hold a note to save my life. I was just pretty much going through the motions; learning the ritual for use later in life. Doing it because that was what was expected. At age 13 I was sent to confirmation classes to memorize scripture and learn all the correct things to say and do.

At age 16 I was asked to fill in for three months for the church secretary who would be out on maternity leave. Eleven years later she still had not returned. Incidentally, I was asked to be church secretary not because of my involvement with the church but because I could type and was under the age of seventy.

During my time as secretary I was made privy to many of the behind-the-scenes workings of the church. I began to realize that this was not only a religious institution, but also a business. That didn't sit well with me. I didn't understand why so much money was being raised for the building fund, the steeple fund, the new narthex fund and on and on. Why didn't we give money every Sunday for the family up the street that the father had been laid off and they were struggling financially? Why didn't we give money to the little girl at school who smelled bad and needed new clothes? Why didn't we give money to the elderly woman who lived near the church and practically froze to death every winter because she needed to save money by turning her heat down to dangerously low temperatures?

I have no beef with God or religion. My problem lies with receiving my information from human beings. There is a party game called "whisper down the lane" in which a group of people stand in a row. Person number one whispers a sentence into the ear of person number two. Person number two tries to repeat the sentence to person number three and so on. When the sentence arrives in the ear of the last person they repeat it out loud and it generally is completely different than the original sentence whispered into the number two person's ear.

The Bible was written by people. The Bible is interpreted by people; lots of different people. Preaching is done by people and, in my opinion, all the information is then slightly skewed by the fact that a human being is interpreting it. I will make my own decisions and formulate my own opinions on what right and wrong are by listening to the little voice in my heart.

My father used to use the term "Sunday morning Christians" to categorize the folks that went to church on Sunday morning and then treated their fellow human beings horribly the rest of the week. They come away from their Sunday morning worship service absolved of all sin because they had their weekly Sunday morning religious "shower." I watched as some of the Elders of the church would light up their cigars outside after the service. Hey…wait a minute…I thought the body was a temple! I watched as some of the Elders tried to get one family shunned from the church because they didn't have money to give, smelled bad, and their children were slightly slow and not very pretty to look at. The aforementioned family was treated like lepers by many in the congregation.

I, myself, got treated to some of the Elders hospitality one Sunday morning. My parents were going to miss this particular Sunday's service and had asked if I could provide a floral arrangement for the coffee hour that was to take place at the end of the regular church service. Coffee hour took place once a month and was to serve as a time to gather and socialize. My mother was responsible for the floral arrangement and didn't want to shun her duties and thusly passed them on to me. I went to our local florist Saturday morning and dutifully chose a beautiful arrangement of flowers for the next morning's service.

The next morning I arrive at church and place my arrangement in the kitchen—as my mother had instructed—and went to take my seat for the service. About a half an hour later, midway through the sermon, one of the Elder-women came in through the back of the church and tapped me on the shoulder. "Where are the nuts and mints?" she questioned in a barely hushed whisper with a tight-lipped expression on her face. I was dumbfounded. My brain scrambled to switch gears from the calming and inspirational sermon I had been roused from to try and grasp what the hell this woman was talking about. I almost dropped my cranial transmission right there on the pew trying to switch gears that quickly. "What nuts and mints?" I finally managed to sputter. "The person responsible for the floral arrangement is *also* responsible for providing nuts and mints. Now we won't have any nuts and mints for the coffee hour" she snapped in an annoyed whisper that could be heard about ten pews away. She then exited the back of the church in a huff. (You had to exit in the back of the church and go around the outside to get into the church's kitchen.)

I sat for a stunned moment trying to wrap my brain around what had just happened. I decided that instead of causing this woman an aneurism I would just run and purchase some nuts and mints. I slithered out of the church like a woman with a scarlet letter on my breast and hot-footed it to the local grocery store.

I returned to the church with my nuts and mints in hand. I walked into the kitchen and deposited my nuts and mints on the counter in front of the group of women who had spent the entire church service preparing for the unbelievably important coffee hour. They all looked surprised and some a little embarrassed. I never went to church again.

I don't believe I am going to hell because I don't go to church. If God is real, I find it hard to believe he is going to send me to hell for not getting up on Sunday morning and driving to a building that man made and listening to right and wrong in a man's opinion. I try to do the right thing every day and I commune with God and the Universe on a daily basis as I watch a heron gliding in for a landing in the creek behind my house. I commune with my conscience every day as I ask myself to examine my motives every time I want to go ballistic on someone who has caused me irritation.

Many religious leaders are right up there with politicians in my opinion. They may have started out with the right intentions, but power has gone to their heads. Their innate humanness has gotten in the way of their originally intended good deeds.

All of the stories of priests molesting young children have saddened me. All of the scenes I've witnessed of the thumping of a preachers' hand on a pulpit to induce his congregation to give, give, give only to find out he is driving a Mercedes and lives in a mansion with a pool have angered me. All of the religious leaders spouting "thou shalt not" only to find out that they "shalt" have jaded me to the point of total faith in God and the Universe and zero faith in my religious and/or political leaders.

I recently finished a book that was given to me by one of my cleaning client's to use as entertainment on a plane trip. The book is called *The Shack.* If you have not read this book yet and have the same types of doubts and concerns I do about the world of religion; you should get this book…read this book…let it sink in and then really think on it.

The author is William Paul Young and he has written a truly thought-provoking book and I wish every single word of it were true. If everything in this book were true it would make sense of the senseless, explain the unexplainable, right all the wrongs and turn the world right-side-up for me.

The ideas in this book would allow all of the meanderings and questions in my mind to stop. A pure truth could be made of my jaded thoughts and damaged wishes.

*"The only tyrant I accept in this world is the still voice within."*
*—Mahatma Gandhi*

# Dinosaurs and Aliens

My mother is one of the nicest, most giving, honest, and decent human beings I have ever known and probably ever will know. My father is an equally decent person although he is not quite as selfless as my mother, but close. My parents have worked their behind's off throughout their entire lives and don't have a whole lot to show for it because they are always helping someone else. Every time they get a little money in their hands they find someone worse off and wind up giving it away. I want them to be comfortable and secure during the retirement years and sometimes get frustrated with just how selfless they are, but deep down I have more respect for them than probably just about anyone else in the world.

Having given the appropriate praise, now to the real topic. My mother. She and I have had many interesting conversations over the years, but some stayed with me more than others. One of the most interesting and memorable conversations we had was a multi-hour debate over religion. She is a deeply religious and faithful person. I love that about her. She can give her all to something without having any proof. We were discussing the Bible and Christian history when I asked her "How do you squeeze the millions of years that the dinosaurs were here *before* Man ever showed up with the beginning of the Bible and 'God created heaven and Earth in six days and on the seventh he rested'?" I thought she would have no answer to this except pure faith. I should have known better. She said "Who knows how long a day is. A day could be one hundred million years." Ok.

Another question I asked was "Do you believe in extraterrestrials?". If God created heaven and Earth, what about life on other planets? Is it possible that in this vast universe we are the only planet with living beings. Once again she had an answer. She said that all of the stories of humans being abducted by the gray-green "aliens" with large black eyes and two long fingers can be explained. The aliens that so many claim to have seen are actually *us* time traveling back from the future. We have advanced technologically to the point where we can time travel and keep traveling back to check on ourselves. We have developed into the pasty gray-green colored folks due to our time constantly spent inside under fluorescent lights. We have those large black eyes and two long fingers because of our time spent on computers. We sit and stare at computers so much that our eyes needed to become enlarged. We spent so much time with our hands perched on our computer mouses with only two fingers—the index and middle fingers—in use therefore those two fingers have extended and the rest have just disappeared.

The drawings of the alleged aliens generally show a slender, non-muscular body. She feels this is because our technology has spoiled us. We no longer need to be physically strong which has caused our bodies to change. Our muscles have atrophied and our brains have enlarged.

At first glance this theory sounds like that of a person not quite in touch with reality, but if you give yourself the opportunity to ponder it…really envision where we currently are in our history, it doesn't sound so crazy. How many of us are sitting for hours upon hours in our office cubicles with our eyes riveted on the computer screen and our right hand lovingly embracing the key to our lifeline …the computer mouse. How many parts of our bodies are being utilized in this atmosphere: two fingers, our brains, our eyes.

I must admit that I find my mother's theory on aliens much more comforting than the Will Smith version in "Men in Black." I would prefer to think that the pasty green guys constantly haunting our cow pastures and bedrooms are there to check on us and help us continue on the road to survival instead of thinking they are here to experiment on us like a scientist with his troop of white mice running through a maze with the eventual ending of them taking over our planet, sucking out our brains, or enslaving us as their proverbial oxen.

What is the majority of science anyway…theory. I know there are broad thinking people throughout history who have made wilder claims only to be proven correct. I am not saying that I believe my mother's theories. I am just saying that the worst thing you can do in life is close your mind to possibility. Remember, the world was *flat* at one time.

*"It is not important what you believe, only that you believe."*
*—Unknown author*

*"Imagination is more important than knowledge. Knowledge is limited. Imagination encircles the world."*
*—Albert Einstein*

# Save The Tantrums

I spent the first years of my young adult life trying to harness a wicked temper. Early on, while dating my now ex-husband, I recall a perfect example of my misplaced temper. We were with a group of people (I didn't use the term friends because his best friend was the biggest jerk I had met to that point in life).

Two of my friends that were at this restaurant/bar were also coworkers. The male coworker was a mild-mannered, nice guy who was desperately in love with my female coworker-friend. He was always nothing but polite and sweet and patient. Too nice. Sometimes nice guys really do finish last.

Anyway, my ex-husband's nasty friend was hitting on my female coworker-friend simply because he *knew* the male coworker-friend really liked her. He was crude and obnoxious and spoiled the entire evening for everyone. My ex-husband thought the whole thing was hilarious which brought about a tongue-lashing in my best fit of Irish temper and concluded with me storming out of the establishment with just about the entire place watching.

What I didn't realize at the time was that my rash behavior was more than likely more embarrassing than the original problem. My temper explosion didn't change a thing about the situation. I had not solved anything. All I had done was given a bully the satisfaction of getting a rise out of me. It took me years to realize that people like that love to shock and upset the sensibilities of nicer people. They feed on causing negative feelings.

Time and time again I would explode at what I felt were injustices inflicted upon others. I somehow thought it was my place to become avenger for all the quieter, nicer people of the world. Whenever I perceived an injustice I would don my cape and tights and let the shit hit the fan.

In all those years and during all those so-called rescues, I never actually helped anyone that I am aware of. I just exacerbated the situations. As I got older I realized that I needed to stop trying to make everyone be nice and get along. I needed to stop trying to make everyone do the right thing because there is only one person I can control…myself. I needed to quit working on everyone else and work on myself. I still come across people acting in a way that cause my "hackles to stand up," but now I try take a minute to take a breath and control my reaction instead of trying to control their action (most of the time…big, big grin). They are responsible for their actions and I am responsible for mine.

*"The proud man hath no God; the envious man hath no neighbor; the angry man hath not himself."*
*—Joseph Hall*

# The Power of Positive Thinking

I love the quote "He who has begun is already half-finished." I have just altered it to pertain to me; "*She* who has begun is already half finished."

The power of positive thinking has been touted by many a "Mary Sunshine." I will admit to being a "Mary Sunshine." Reading this book could give the impression that I am interested in nothing more than being bitchy and judgmental. No so!

While I do have an opinion on just about everything, I am also a perpetually-perky-person, to the annoyance of just about everyone I know. If I had a dollar for every time someone rolled their eyes at my search for the silver lining in every situation, I would be a millionaire.

I totally believe that a deliberate positive or negative mindset can make all the difference in the world in someone's life. I love to whine and complain about things, however, then I try to purposefully stop that train of thought and replace it with an opposite outlook. Whenever I feel myself slipping down the slippery slope to self-pity, I verbally (out loud) chastise myself and steer the train away from the pity party toward something a little more productive. I am sure my audible chastising is quite a sight for the strangers witnessing it.

A prime example of my purposeful thinking is the story of why and how I own two lawn mowers. These are popular lawn mowers because they are also used in my "women are crazy" area of this book.

I have a complicated-to-use and complicated-to-upkeep mulching mower and I have a simplistic reel mower. My complicated mulching mower is heavy and hard to push therefore it has a self-propulsion system. After you are ready to go, you pull a handle and the mower pulls itself along; you are just there as the steering mechanism. One day the self-propulsion thingy quit working and pushing this heavy beast up my back hill was virtually impossible.

Since I had been thinking for quite a while of getting one of the old-fashioned reel mowers to get away from using gasoline to mow my yard—which is not that big—I took the mulching mower to get repaired and purchased a reel mower. My checking account had $144.06 in it at the time of the reel mower purchase. The reel mower bill was $143.05. If you can do the math, that left me with $1.01 in my checking account.

Money has always been tight, however, I don't stress as much as one might think because I swear to you that I put my needs out into the universe and my needs always seem to be met.

Instead of crying that I only have $1.01 left over after buying the mower (which was necessary as the complicated mower was broken), I came out of the mower shop with a grin on my face because I had skated through again. I didn't have *only* $1.01 left…I had a *whole* $1.01 left! I didn't overdraw my account. I had money left over! Woooo hoooo!

Another time I was struggling financially was just after my ex-husband and I had just separated. Money was *really* tight. I was doing my best to stretch a dollar as far as it would go and we were doing ok, but sometimes I had to skip purchasing little things like groceries! One week in particular I remember paying the electric bill and realizing there would be no money left over for groceries. Oh well, it's not like we'll starve. Most American households have enough food in the cabinets to last for a month. We need to go to the store because what we *have* in our cabinets in not what we *want*. There is a big difference between *want* and *need*. So I decided we could forego purchasing any groceries that week.

I had been a youth soccer coach for about eleven years at this time and really loved it. I loved coming up with ways to bring the shy kids out of their shell, developing strategies for building confidence in the kids and helping the little guys stay healthy and active. I always felt great after running around the fields with my players; endorphins pulsing through me. I am a hugely competitive person, but youth sports need to be about the bigger picture; making a well-rounded human being.

Anyway, the week before the grocery mini-crisis we had just ended our spring soccer season. As always, it had been a fun season and I was going to miss the kids and the parents I had gotten to know and love.

The day of the bill-paying and grocery mini-crisis I had completed all of my bookwork, picked the kids up from school and grabbed the mail on our way in the driveway. Once inside the house, I sat down at my desk to go through the mail. A small pink envelope immediately caught my eye because it was personal, unlike most of the junk mail that I am inundated with every day (which could be another topic; junk mail should be illegal). I opened the pink envelope and it contained a very thoughtful thank you note signed by all of the parents and players from my spring soccer team. The note also included a gift card to our local grocery store. Wow, the Universe works fast! I didn't even know you could buy gift cards from the grocery store. Who would even *think* to purchase a gift card from the grocery store.

I have so many instances of this type that I could never remember them all or have enough paper and ink to relate them all to others. I relay these few to hopefully get people to start calming all the "white noise" in their lives and get back to their roots. Connect to the Universe and feel the calming effect of full faith that what is *needed* will be provided. What is *wanted*...well...you are on your own.

*"Nothing can stop the man with the right mental attitude from achieving his goal; nothing on earth can help the man with the wrong mental attitude."*
*—Thomas Jefferson*

*"A pessimist is one who makes difficulties of his opportunities and an optimist is one who makes opportunities of his difficulties."*
*—Harry S. Truman*

*"Don't believe in miracles—depend on them."*
*—Laurence J. Peter*

# Embrace Your Defects

We are constantly inundated by commercials on our television sets about all the medications we need to fix, get rid of, or otherwise control all of our problems. We are lemmings. We believe all the caca the advertisers are shoveling and pay top dollar for the caca. Day in and day out we stand at the edge of the cliff and follow these advertisements over the edge. We need to become free thinking lemmings. Lemmings who enjoy our kinship to our fellow human beings, but don't feel the need to jump off the cliff just because Bob and Earl Lemming jumped off. I've often wondered if we hadn't heard of half our ailments if we would have actually developed them independently. In other words, what came first, the chicken or the egg? Did we have the ailment first or did we develop the ailment *after* hearing about it. Never underestimate the power of suggestion.About two months after seeing my first commercial for restless leg syndrome, my entire household has it. Everyone complains about their legs feeling funny at night. I am forty-one years old and have never felt this restless leg feeling before. Now all the sudden some nights when I go to bed I have to curl my legs up as they feel funny and I can't seem to get comfortable due to the feeling that I need to keep moving them. Damn, I knew I should have demolished all the "boob tubes" in my house. Boob tube is my dad's name for television. He calls it that because he says that watching television is making us all stupid, i.e. boobs.

There are genuine health issues that need medication. There are genuine mental issues that need to be dealt with. It just seems to me there are some problems that we could work on ourselves and other so-called problems that we should just embrace.

As for myself, I believe I'm hyperactive. As a child, my mother used to reach over and place a hand over mine to stop my tapping or place a hand on my knee to stop the foot wiggling. I talked nonstop and incessantly about anything and everything (still do). I am so glad my mother just dealt with me instead of medicating me. One of my teachers placed me in the front of the classroom so she could tap my desk when she saw that my mind was wandering to the bug crawling up the window or the fascinating speck on my desk top. I did find a way around the teachers' solution of putting me in front near her desk. I could amuse myself for a really long time with a pretty little Avon ring my mother had given me. It was a fake ruby ring that had a very flat surface to the "ruby." I could pretend to be resting my head on my fisted hand and be listening to the teacher when I was really looking at what was going on out the window as it was reflected in the rings' flat surface. I could see who was playing with whom at recess, who was hanging upside down on the monkey bars with their underwear sticking out and who was ticking off the ladies in charge of the students at recess. A whole world on the small surface of a fake ruby ring.

Actually, I don't know if I was that different from other children. Most kids have the attention span of a gnat. I always thought it was perfectly normal. I have coached youth soccer for fourteen years and the biggest bit of knowledge I have gained in all these years is DO NOT have small children standing in a line. They will inevitably be tapping the person in front of them or poking the person behind them, squashing bugs on their forehead, picking wedgies or noses, and by the time their turn arrives, they have no idea what they are supposed to be doing. Keeping *all* players engaged at *all* times is paramount.

Should they all be medicated because they have the attention span of a gnat? Or for some of them should we just adjust the way we teach so as to engage their minds…a lot of the time. I know there are real circumstances when medication is called for to raise the quality of life for some who really can't learn or focus, but I also think medications make things too easy. We could maybe work a little harder sometimes.

I have embraced my hyperness. I have found that I get more done in a days' time than most people do in a week! I have learned to make chronological lists of what I need to do each day to keep myself organized because my mind does tend to wander. My friend's call it the "Look there's a chicken" syndrome. Their little saying means that I can be talking, in depth, on a topic and if something else catches my attention I will switch subjects mid-sentence without so much as a breath. I usually get back on topic eventually; much like this book.

My hyperness has allowed me to be super-productive and energetic. I like that about myself and the people close to me have learned to appreciate my active-quirkiness. I prefer to call my hyperness "active-quirkiness"; just sounds more positive.

Another area my "active-quirkiness" has been an advantage to me is coaching youth soccer. It has been so rewarding. I have met a multitude of people that I would not otherwise have gotten to know. I have felt the joy of teaching something to a child and watching them execute it perfectly in a game. I have watched confidence being built and self-esteem being established in kids; and hopefully in some way I helped them to gain a little of those all-important traits.

My "active-quirkiness" has given me the energy to run around at practices multiple times per week with human beings thirty years younger than myself and keep up. It has given me the inspiration to stand on a side line jumping up and down chattering constantly to my little players on how fabulous, excellent, phenomenal they are and what a great job they are doing. I am the loudest person at the field when it comes time for our team cheer and the kids love it. I feel the only reason I have been able to be a small part of helping so many kids find their confidence and esteem is because of my "active-quirkiness." Why would I want to medicate it away?

There is also a benefit that I am sure many people haven't thought of with "active-quirkiness"; I save money. There's no need for drugs and alcohol to be the loudest and most obnoxious person at a party. I never have to worry about driving home from a party drunk or winding up wandering naked through a mall because I am high. I don't *need* any of that stuff to constantly be on the move, having fun, and being obnoxious. So, if you would prefer to have one loud, obnoxious person at your party that you don't have to drive home at the end of the night or clean up your bathroom floor after they have spewed the hors d'ouerves…invite me!

If you ask my children they will say there is a down-side to my energy level. I don't drink coffee or soda or need caffeine of any kind to bound out of bed at 6:00 a.m. every day and poke, tickle and harass them to get up for school. They would probably appreciate a little medication coming my way in order to stop me from jumping up and down on their beds to vibrate them over the edge onto the floor.

I have never been formally diagnosed, but believe myself to be obsessive/compulsive also. Since childhood I have been obsessed with spelling things. I hear a word or phrase and spell it out in my head over and over. Not only do I have to spell things over and over, but I have to spell them in rhythm. An example would be the word "spelling." I would spell it in groups of two letters…sp-el-li-ng. Oh goodie! It comes out evenly. There are eight letters in the word "spelling" and so it can be spelled beautifully over and over in groups of two letters at a time. Now let's take the word "beautiful." Be-au-ti-fu-l….aaaahhhhh…there are nine letters in the word "beautiful" so it can't be spelled perfectly in groups of two. This calls for drastic measures. In the case of odd numbered words like "beautiful," I start with a group of one letter so it can end perfectly…b-ea-ut-if-ul. That's better.

After taking typing class in high school, I also started to not only do these random and methodical spellings in my head, but I also envisioned a typewriter and actually typed the words in my head. Scary, isn't it?

This is just the tip of the iceberg to my obsessive/compulsiveness, however, I am looking at the bright side. I am a GREAT speller. I am methodical about the way I choose to do things. I have developed into a high speed typist, which is how I got the job typing manuscripts, which is how I got the job typing Kenny Maynes' book, which is what inspired me to write my own. So, I am sitting in *this* chair, typing *this* book, on *this* day and totally enjoying myself because I have issues. Ain't life grand?

I am admittedly *very* anal which has translated into a successful cleaning business and actually, success at any job I have done. I have not tried to relax so I can "drop my load" once a day like most people. I embrace my analness which allows me to do a good job for the people I work for. It allows me to be very organized and on top of things. If I feel the need to "drop a load"… I will just eat more raisin bran that morning. I know…that was disgusting.

I never realized until right now…writing this chapter that all of the jobs I have had revolved around me organizing and "cleaning up" behind someone. I started with a banking job right out of high school. I ran a computer system. This job called for a lot of energy and organization. I spent time as an assistant to a large retail store manager. She cried when I quit. I worked at a hair salon scheduling all of the haircuts, keeping the ten, young and impetuous female hairstylists from killing each other, and doing the books and deposits at the end of the night. I then worked for six years as an assistant to a real estate agent who, previous to me, couldn't keep an assistant for more than six months because he was a MESS! I thrive on the challenge of the impossible.

I am not saying that modern medicine is all bad. I am not trivializing real problems that people are suffering from. I am just saying that we don't *always* need a pill to resolve what ails us; or what society *perceives* as an ailment. I think that saying "One man's trash is another man's treasure" applies nicely here; one man's ailment is another man's gift.

*"Life's blows cannot break a person whose spirit is warmed at the fire of enthusiasm."*
*—Norman Vincent Peale*

*"None are so old as those who have outlived enthusiasm."*
*—Henry David Thoreau*

# Post-Separation Dating, My Ocean Is Now A Puddle

On my thirty-eighth birthday I became a newly separated woman. Yikes! I had spent the past seventeen years with one man and had four children with him. I spent my days working part-time, changing diapers, feeding children, teaching children their ABC's and 123's, and just generally being a mom. I love being a mom.

On day one of the separation I did a naked happy-dance on my deck around 5:30 a.m. (a symbol of liberation), then scrubbed the house from top to bottom to get rid of his cooties (a symbol of immaturity), and then stood staring at the black hole of the future of my love life. "I will be alone forever because no one will ever want a stretch-marked, graying, sagging, wrinkling, premenopausal thirty-eight year old mother of four.

Contemplating the possibility of being alone for the rest of my life brought me to the conclusion that it wouldn't be so bad. I had a feeling of freedom for the first time in my adult life. I was no longer at the mercy of someone else's whims. I no longer had to ask for every penny I spent and fork over every penny I earned. I breathed. I breathed very deeply and unrestricted. It felt good. So what if I would no longer have a significant other. I finally was proud of myself and truly liked who I had grown into. I was finally feeling strong and in control. I didn't have two pennies to rub together, but when and if I did acquire two pennies to rub together I could do whatever I wanted with them. I would rather be captain of a dinghy than a prisoner on a yacht. My life as a mother was extremely rewarding. I was involved in every aspect of my children's lives and had no shortage of things to keep me occupied. The prospect's were endless. Besides, my oldest son who was about 15 years old at the time informed me that my chances of dating were slim so I should get used to being alone. He said that I wasn't hideous or anything, but when I was younger there was an entire ocean of companion choices, but now as I was pushing forty years old, I only had a puddle of companion choices left. Ain't kids sweet!? Believe it or not, he meant well.

Prior to the separation I had planned on continuing to work at the real estate office as an assistant and fill out my schedule with also working for the office mortgage consultant. It was all worked out and ready to go. During the days after the separation I checked with the mortgage consultant who then informed me that the job wasn't quite ready yet. There was more paperwork to do and the laptop wasn't quite set up for me and on and on. The job wouldn't be ready for me for another two months. WHAT!? My children and I will be starving and living in a cardboard box in two months. I need money NOW!

I have learned many, many life lessons along the way and here was the opportunity to catalogue another one. Go with the flow. You never know what tomorrow will bring.

I immediately went into a spiraling panic. Once I stopped and took a deep breath I decided that I would just find some job…any job…until the mortgage job was ready. I opened up my local newspaper and called about the first job I saw. A cleaning company was looking for help. $10 an hour. I called and started two days later.

Let me stop here to give a little more background on my issues. I am a neat person. I like things just so. I like all the towels hung up with edges perfectly straight and no tags showing. I like my faucets wiped and polished to a high shine. One of my favorite sayings to my children when I wake them for school in the morning is, "A made bed is a happy bed." OK…back to the story. I started working immediately for the cleaning business and realized very quickly that I was good at this job. I loved to clean. I totally loved the working environment. I showed up at a house in shorts, t-shirt, and sneakers. Turned on a radio—that I had previously procured permission to use from the homeowners—and then proceeded to mindlessly clean and organize the house. The sense of accomplishment each day of going into a house that was dirty and unorganized and leaving it with everything in its place and the sun sparkling off every surface was so satisfying. By the time the mortgage consultant called me two months later to say that the job was ready, I had managed to get quite a few houses of my own and had quit working for the cleaning business. Instead of $10 an hour working for someone else I had found my own clients and was making double per house. I eventually acquired some commercial businesses to clean as well. Business was booming and the kids and I were not going to have to live in a cardboard box. Life was good.

The point of this story is that my life went in a totally different direction than I thought it would. The job crisis had resolved itself and was actually better than my original plan. I made more money cleaning than I could have ever made at the real estate office. I could pick and choose the houses and businesses I would clean. The days and times I chose to work were totally up to me. I could make a living and still be home for the kids before school and after school. I could go to their games and deliver them to all extracurricular activities without fear of reproach from a boss. It was and still is perfect.

This perfection in my work/parenting situation gave me a sense of fulfillment that helped me to realize that I could be perfectly happy without a significant other. My life was full and felt very complete.

Funny how life works; as soon as I found confidence and strength in myself men started coming out of the woodwork asking me out. All of the chaos and baggage that came with my life didn't seem to matter. Suddenly, I was irresistible to men of all ages and walks of life. I had an older gentleman follow me out of the grocery store to offer me his phone number. I had a younger guy somewhere in his late twenties or early thirties showing real interest. I don't know his age because we didn't get very far into getting to know each other. He was living on a different planet than I was. He had never been married and had no children. I felt he and I would have had nothing in common…well…nothing except the fact that he was blonde, blue-eyed, gorgeous and built like a brick house…

Sorry, I got lost there for a minute (grin). I had a photographer trick me into giving him my phone number while my daughter, who was doing local modeling at the time, was being photographed. It was amazing. However, I never actually went on a date. Something just wasn't quite right with each possible romantic situation.

Finally, a year and a half after separating I stumbled onto a golden opportunity. It was early December and I had taken a Friday off to do some Christmas shopping. I was just completing my shopping at one particular store. While pushing my cart around the final corner heading for the checkout area I glanced up and my eyes met these clear blue eyes. My brain quickly summarized… "cute"…but my feet kept moving toward the long checkout line. A few minutes later I hear a voice behind me, "Did you find everything you were looking for?" I turned toward the voice and standing there was this 6'4" gorgeous man with strawberry-blonde curly hair, clear blue eyes, and an amazing smile. I said something stupid like "No, I couldn't find a tablecloth for my square table." There was a little bit more small talk about the tablecloth quandary and then I thanked him and he walked away.

After standing in the long line for what seemed like forever, it was finally my turn. I flopped all my items onto the counter as a woman came in the door holding a baby with one shoe. This particular December day was frigid and extremely blustery. This frazzled woman asked my clerk if anyone had jumper cables as her car had died and she and the baby were freezing. My clerk raised her head and called to the blonde Adonis who had chatted with me earlier. She used his first name. Ah-ha! He is not only nice and gorgeous, but now I know his first name. The Blonde Adonis and the woman with the baby with one shoe then disappeared.

I completed my purchase and headed out of the store. Standing right in front of my totally cool, white mini-van full of kid junk was the blonde Adonis and the lady with the baby with one shoe. I offered help, but he said he was going to get her a battery and install it from a store just blocks away.

I then proceeded to back out of my parking space as the blonde Adonis stood smiling at me with one hand up in a casual good-bye wave.

WHAT is the matter with me. This guy *obviously* had interest and *I* was obviously interested, yet, like a seventh grade girl at the junior high dance, I just kept going.

I arrived at my next stop which was a store where I purchased my Christmas cards. I sat in my van for fifteen minutes admonishing myself for being so shy and childish. What is the worst thing that would happen if I told this guy he had a great smile? So, I opened the box of Christmas cards, wrote a quick note stating I liked his smile and included only my first name and cell phone number. I wrote his first name on the outside of the envelope. Remember I had gained his first name from the clerk calling out to him.

I drove back to the store full of boldness and confidence, then proceeded to slink through the store hiding behind racks and shelves until reaching the customer service counter. My boldness and confidence deserted me the second I reentered the store. I handed the envelope to the customer service attendant and high-tailed it out of the store. I felt like I was a spy on a top secret mission and had just escaped detection. Phew!

Half an hour later the blonde Adonis phoned me and we decided to meet the next day at a neutral location to talk. We have been together three years now. As a side bonus he is also a licensed massage therapist. Could life get any better?

Like I said… life is funny…you just never know what is around each corner so DO NOT let a tough situation or bad day drag you down. Tomorrow is another day and there could be a million dollar lottery ticket or a blonde Adonis waiting around tomorrow's corner. Or there could be just another beautiful day to watch a butterfly flit by and enjoy your own company. Love yourself, get comfortable in your own skin, and anything on top of that is just icing on the cake.

*"It is better to conquer yourself than to win a thousand battles. Then the victory is yours. It cannot be taken from you, not by angels or by demons, heaven or hell."*
*—Buddha*

# Money: Curse or Blessing?

I recently watched a documentary on our public broadcast station about Eleanor Roosevelt. I have a watercolor that sits prominently on my computer desk with an Eleanor Roosevelt quote printed on it; "A woman is like a teabag. You never know how strong she is until she gets into hot water." I was given this watercolor by a fiery, Irish, Gemini friend of mine (big grin) during the months immediately after my separation when my confidence was flagging. I placed this watercolor and quote in a prominent place as I wanted to read it every day as an affirmation; A way to remind myself that "I am woman, hear me roar."

Due to the few tidbits I had learned about Eleanor Roosevelt over the years and this empowering quote that had become a part of my daily life, I thought of Eleanor Roosevelt as this amazingly strong, confident—not to mention wealthy—woman. I envied her strength and determination and most definitely the wealth she had access to.

The public broadcast program I watched about her life was very enlightening. She had been born into a very wealthy family. She was surrounded by the privilege and excess that tons of money can buy...yet...

As the program progressed I became more and more appreciative of the simple middle class life I lived. Eleanor had an alcoholic father, a mother who cared about nothing but the girls looks because that is how she felt women were judged. Beauty was the only asset worth anything and Eleanor fell short of her mother's expectations. What a sad, lonely girl she appeared to be in every photograph of her childhood years.

Her parents both died very young and she was sent to live with her grandmother. In her grandmother's home she had to be locked into her room to ward off the alcoholic and lecherous uncles. She was eventually sent to boarding school overseas. At the conclusion of this program I had seen a multitude of photo's and film footage of this woman. I believe that I saw her smile three or four times. The depth of sadness in her eyes and body language was downright depressing.

Let's examine what we know. This woman was born with a silver spoon in her mouth and struggled every day of her life with self-confidence, self-esteem, and self-loathing. She had no real family ties that were healthy.

I think the miracle here is not that she was fortunate enough to have been born into a family with a lot of money; the miracle is she survived it and became the icon we all know and love *despite* being wealthy.

I see examples each day of why being physically attractive, having a lot of money, or having all the latest material gadgets do *not* assure happiness. It almost seems that in some instances these things can actually be a curse. Be careful what you wish for.

In another use of the word *Perfection*, I want to remind people to not only avoid being envious of perceived perfection in others, but also to not expect perfection in those we view to be less than perfect. Boy, that was a mouthful.

What I mean by that is we all have imperfections and need to take a step back once in a while to look in the mirror before pointing a finger at another. I am a smoker. I am not proud, but also not ashamed. I picked the habit up at a very young age. I was in grade school the first time I pilfered one of my dad's non-filter camels. I loved the taste from the very first one. I didn't stick with the non-filter because I didn't like the feel of the little bits of tobacco stuck to my tongue, but I did continue the habit. Am I advocating smoking? No, certainly not. Am I thrilled that I smoke? No, I wish I had never started. I wish I had never started because smoking is unhealthy and expensive. I do, however, still enjoy it which is why I haven't quit.

I bring up this subject because I have been harassed enumerable times about being a smoker and it astounds me that some of the folks doing the harassing can't see their own imperfections.

I worked in the real estate industry for eleven years. The office I worked at had a sales meeting every Tuesday morning. We would discuss changes in the industry, new laws, and new listings that our company had picked up. At the conclusion of every sales meeting all of the agents would pile into a few cars and hit the road to tour all of the new listings so we could accurately speak about them to potential clients. We needed to see the product in order to effectively sell it.

As each sales meeting was wrapping up, I would slip out to get a cigarette in before all of the other agents were packed into the vehicles and ready to leave. There were about four of us smokers who had to stick together. We had our little designated area outside and we huddled together like lepers. On one occasion an obnoxious agent from our office marched up to me and said "Oh, you're one of *those*." My mind was racing. One of those…one of WHAT?! What did he mean by one of those…a woman…Irish…brown-eyed…WHAT?

I asked him to clarify what he meant. He said "A smoker" and then proceeded to clue me in on all of the health risks and how unattractive it made me. Being attractive to this particular man was not something I, or any of womankind, should aspire to. He was an arrogant jerk.

I calmly told him that I was well aware of the health risks and if he found it so unattractive, he could kindly move to a more attractive area of the out-of-doors. Then I finished with something like "I know what you mean about unhealthy and unattractive because that is exactly what I think of that huge spare tire you carry around your middle from lack of exercise and too many twinkies." He never spoke to me again.

Once again I am not advocating smoking. I am just trying to wake people up to the fact that no one is perfect. The next time you are feeling close to perfect sit down and write a list of *your* bad habits. Take this list with you each time you feel the need to blast someone else for their imperfections. If you subscribe to regular road rage, are racist, are selfish, are a stressed out workaholic, are overweight from bad eating habits and lack of exercise you need to look in the mirror and realize that ALL bad habits are unhealthy and unattractive. I don't smoke indoors. I don't smoke in my own house. No one else needs to be subject to my bad habit. So what is my crime? I have a bad habit and so does the rest of American society. So, I guess what I really want to say to people who want to trash respectful smokers is…well…I can't really say what I want to so I will just let your imaginations run wild.

I really digressed on this one. I started out with the topic of money being a curse or a blessing and ended with how annoying it is when others try to invade your bubble. Sorry for the straying, but I'm going to leave it this way (big grin).

To wrap up my original topic: Benjamin Franklin turned rags to riches through the workings of his mind. He began life with no money, only drive and determination and the gift of his mind. Eleanor Roosevelt started out with a silver spoon in her mouth that practically gagged the life out of her. She overcame through drive and determination and the gift of her mind. Money is neither a curse nor a blessing. The curse or blessing is what you do with your gifts.

*"God gave me my money. I believe the power to make money is a gift from God…to be developed & used to the best of our ability for the good of mankind. Having been endowed with the gift I possess, I believe it is my duty to make money & still more money & to use the money I make for the good of my fellow man according to the dictates of my conscience."*
*—John D. Rockefeller*

*"Let us realize that the privilege to work is a gift, that power to work is a blessing, that love of work is success."*
*—David O. McKay*

*"I'm a great believer in luck and I find the harder I work, the more I have of it."*
*—Thomas Jefferson*

# Talk Is Not Cheap

When I was young and we had a thunderstorm that caused a power outage we had a blast! We lit candles, played hide-and-seek in the house, played board games, or—as astounding as it sounds—we just talked. No television, no radio, no white noise. As an adult I get a feeling of excitement and happiness every time I hear that first rumble of thunder, see that first lightning strike, and feel that first bloated drop of rain. Thunderstorm rain is the best…those drops of water are big enough to fell a moose! There was a wonderful feeling of togetherness and time seems to move so much slower when the outside world gets turned off for awhile. We had a large old farmhouse with a gigantic wrap-around porch. We would sit and just watch and listen to the storm. Aaaaah…life was good. It is really difficult finding that kind of peace in the harried and hurried world of today. What a shame.

*"If we could see the miracle of a single flower clearly,*
*our whole life would change."*
*—Buddha*

*"My life has no purpose, no direction, no aim,*
*no meaning, and yet I'm happy. I can't figure it out.*
*What am I doing right?"*
*—Charles Schulz*

# Lemming Theory

I have eluded to my "lemming theory" a few times throughout this book. Some of the crazy things I have seen in this world can be easily explained by the lemming theory.

Fashion is example number one. I think back to one particular year and one particular outfit in my youth that completely proves the lemming theory. I owned a pair of purple parachute pants. Parachute pants were those tight pants with tons of zippers all over them and they were made out of this slippy material that was similar to the material parachutes were made out of. You not only wore the goofy pants, but fashion dictated that you also had to wear a belt that was about ten feet long and you wrapped it around your waist and lower hips over and over.

The only thing I am thankful for about this era is that there is no photographic proof that I owned the aforementioned pants and that no permanent physical damage was caused to my body from the falls caused by sliding out of…or off of… all smooth seating. Also, a very close friend of mine had an orange pair of "Hammer Pants". Hammer pants were those pants that made you look like a genie. They were huge and baggy all the way down to the knees. These pants were made famous by MC Hammer, thus the name Hammer Pants. My very close friend denies owning said pants, but his daughter swears she remembers a trip to Six Flags with him wearing these orange pants. He knows who he is…

Fashion is an amazing thing that even the most grounded person can get caught up in. On occasion I watch some fashion shows on TV and as the models saunter down the runway in outfits that I can't imagine anyone ever really wearing and with hairdos that I can't imagine anyone ever sporting, I am reminded that we are just lemmings. We are lemmings who will see some famous person wearing something and within days we will find ourselves at the mall trying to emulate that look. Maybe we do this because we want to belong or fit in or maybe we do this because by emulating that famous person we can somehow cause fame and fortune to come our way.

When I think back over the fashion statements made by Boy George, Madonna, Liberace, Elvis, and countless other celebrities, I realize that there are a few individuals and the rest of us race toward the cliffs' edge to jump off and follow their lead. I just thank my lucky stars that I survived my youthful lemming phase without too many photographs as evidence of my lack of individuality (or good taste of any kind).

Another event that comes to mind that completely proves my lemming theory is the Cabbage Patch Doll. All of the sudden on one crazy day all of humanity simultaneously lost their minds. Perfectly normal people went from working at their jobs, taking care of their families, eating their dinners and sleeping at night to waiting frantically in lines and trying to "get the jump on" their friends and neighbors to acquire a Cabbage Patch Doll. Have you seen these dolls? If you have…have you actually looked closely at them? They are babies that look like they have been sucking lemons. They aren't even cute!

As further proof of the lemming mentality, think about religion. There are many religions scattered all over the world. Of these many religions there are still more gods, goddesses and prominent figures being worshipped. Look back through history at all of the worshipped figures and think about this: Can they *all* be real? It just doesn't seem possible that they were or are all real. Yet, there they are. Why so many gods, goddesses, deities, and figures to worship? Because there is a deep-seated need in human beings to believe in something, to put our faith in something, to *follow* something.

We have all sat shaking our heads in amazement at the blind followers of cults. These cult members were asked to do things that most of us would never consider doing. Why would they do that? The answer is simple: they *need* to. I am sure there are human beings out there that can stand independently of all others. Human beings that don't need the fellowship and support of any other. These superhumans are the lemming leaders. Others unconsciously want to follow people like that because somewhere deep down they feel that that guy knows something they don't. It seems to me that many figures that are worshipped were probably developed by lemming leaders in order to control the behavior of his lemming followers.

Have you ever walked down the street and seen a crowd of people looking up toward the sky or down on the ground at something? You are magnetically pulled toward that situation to see what they are looking at.

I watched perfectly sane people stand in long, tension-filled lines waiting to get the latest or newest beanie baby toy. Astounding. It is a piece of fabric filled with little plastic beads or something, yet here were otherwise ordinary folks standing in a line, up on tippy-toes, goose-necking over the crowd to see how many were left. They were wringing their hands and sweating profusely as they watched each person at the front of the line picking and purchasing the Beanie Baby *they* were waiting to purchase. The fear was palpable as the piles of Beanie Babies dwindled the closer they got to the front of the line. I watched these people standing in lines for hours before the store even opened (I lived down the street from a retail store that sold them).

How do these incredible situations arise? People who lead very normal lives who become temporarily insane when a fad takes center stage. All of the other lemmings are running toward the cliff, and for fear of being left out or missing out on something that everyone else is doing, the solitary lemming begins to run and careens off the cliff with the rest.

By the way, if anyone is still in frantic need of Beanie Babies I think my kids have a tub full sitting somewhere in my basement. They received some during many of the holidays and birthdays during that time. I am sure some of them still have their all-important tags, but a few may be wrinkled or torn. Let me know, I'll hook you up.

*"Once you can accept the universe as matter*
*expanding into nothing that is something, wearing stripes*
*with plaid comes easy."*
*—Albert Einstein*

*"Conformity is the jailer of freedom and the enemy of growth."*
*—John F. Kennedy*

# The Bionic Kidney Stone

Somewhere in the sewer system of my hometown floats a kidney stone…my kidney stone. I want it back.

A few months ago I awoke on a Saturday morning around 6:00 am with pain in my lower back on the left side. I had been through the symptoms of a kidney stone with my ex-husband years ago. I knew what the pain was and I knew what was coming…more pain.

My significant other and I headed for the emergency room and arrived by 7:00 am. By the time we were walking through the door of the emergency room the pain had increased to an almost unbearable level. I was never so happy to see a hospital. This sentiment would change later.

Treatment consisted of pain medication which did not stop the pain, but did dull it enough to lay semi-comfortably in my cubicle in the emergency room. My wonderful significant other stayed by my side, rubbing my back and hair, helped keep my IV tube untangled as I writhed in pain, and chased down the nurse every time I started whining for more pain medication.

I was eventually taken for x-rays to find the stone and determine its size. My nurse, who was a good guy, told me the stone was not that large and I would be fine. My doctor, who saw me for five minutes and stood outside my cubicle at the nurses' station drinking coffee and laughing loudly, came in later and said the stone was good size. Hmmm…is it big…is it little…who cares…they said I can go home. I arrived at 7:00 am and was leaving at noon.

When preparing to leave the hospital, I was given a little funnel with straining wire covering the bottom. This funnel was to be used every time I went to the bathroom to strain my urine and find the stone. I used the strainer for about a week and never found the stone. It was either too small for me to find or it passed some time after I stopped using the strainer. If I had known what that little stone was worth, I would have tried a little harder to retrieve it….had it made into a ring or something.

Months later the bills started rolling in for my three-hour visit to the emergency room. First there was $5,000.00 for the emergency room fee. This was just for using a space in their building. I did have to pay $75.00 at the time I arrived at the hospital. This fee was just to *walk* through the door. Then there was $1,000.00 for the doctor who drank coffee and laughed loudly and annoyingly during my stay. Another $346.00 for the doctor who read the x-rays. Ironcially, the nurse who tried to be helpful—and seemed to be the only one with a clue—didn't send me a bill.

What a broken record this is going to sound like…but…wow…our health care system is a mess. When it costs $7,000.00 for three hours… somebody is getting screwed. For that much money they should have stopped my pain, retrieved the stone and made it bionic or something. My kidney stone should have been juiced up to be able to leap tall buildings, see through concrete, run 100 miles per hour, and be able to save small children in danger.

I am one of the fortunate people with health insurance... not great health insurance…but it's something. I had to pay $5,000.00 of the $7,000.00 of my kidney stone bill and insurance covered the other $2,000.00 (like I said, not great health insurance), but how sad is it to have to decide between your health and money. I have decided that if I feel the symptoms of a kidney stone coming on again, I am getting a bottle of whiskey to kill the pain—using my kitchen colander to strain for the stone—and then I can put my kids through college with the money I saved.

*"We contend that for a nation to try to tax itself into prosperity is like a man standing in a bucket and trying to lift himself up by the handle."*
*—Winston Churchill*

# Angels in the Bathroom

I have long been fascinated by the prospect of angels and ghosts. I have seen so many shows on television about ghosts and had quite a few friends who told me stories about their experiences with ghosts. Do I believe, or don't I?

On the one hand I really *want* to believe. Wouldn't it be wonderful to think that we have guardian angels surrounding us and trying to keep us from harm. I envision these beautiful gossamer beings surrounding me. They all have these radiant faces with kind and loving expressions. They love me and are there to do nothing but protect and care for me. Sigh. That sounds wonderful.

Then on the other hand, the other side of my brain says that having guardian angels could be a little tricky. I envision them having a conversation that goes something like this: "What is she doing now?", "Why in the world does she have to move so fast? I'm exhausted.", "She is not *really* gonna drive through those flood waters!", "If she gets on that dirt bike I am outta here!", "Why doesn't she just *hire* someone to climb up and fix the roof!", "Do you think we could get our assignment switched to the nice, calm lady next door?"

As well as my angels being disappointed and frustrated with my antics, I also worry about other possible problems with having a troop of angels following me. Do they see me looking in the mirror and popping zits? Are they watching as I battle a particularly difficult bout of constipation while shaking their heads and expounding the benefits of eating more fiber? Do they cringe and hold their hands over their ears when my sailor language slips out? And the biggest concern is if my guardian angel is my brother…is he watching as I have sex and thinking what a bad girl I am?!

I have often heard people say they believe that our guardian angels are people we have known, loved and lost throughout our lives. The biggest loss I have felt came when my brother—who battled cancer from about the age of eleven to fourteen—passed away. I have two brothers and this was the brother that actually *liked* me. He was artistic and caring. We fought like normal siblings, yet he had a soft spot for me. He would include me in games of monopoly and throw a kind word my way once in a while. He was four years older than I was so that is saying a lot for a boy that age. It would be a little embarrassing if he was the one assigned to watch over me.

As for ghosts, I have had many interesting conversations on this topic. I personally know many people, whom I consider perfectly sane, who claim to have grown up in a house with ghosts, had ghosts constantly moving things or opening and shutting doors etc. I have not been fortunate enough to have any firsthand experiences, but am intrigued. Like I said earlier, I have two brothers, one still with us and one moved on. The brother that is still with us is a cut-and-dried kind of person. He has a masters' degree in marine biology and is one of those people who seems to know everything (or is really good at pretending he does). He and I had a long conversation one time about religions and ghosts. The closest I could come to an admission from him that it was *possible* was a remark he made about energy. He told me that energy cannot be destroyed. If a human being is alive, thusly having energy, when the body dies the energy has to go *somewhere*. Hmmmm. So there is a distinct possibility that even a clear-headed, solemn scientist has a remote belief in ghosts.

I am not always sure what *exactly* I believe. As I said before, a good argument can sway me.

The only thing I am one hundred percent sure of is…I believe in possibility. I do believe in Kharma because I *want* to believe in Kharma. I want to believe that when someone does something nasty or thoughtless to me that I don't need to walk over and punch them in the face because somewhere down the road the Universe will take care of it for me. I believe you get what you give and if you give good, good will come back to you and if you give negativity, negativity will come back to you…eventually.

Also, if my brother is to be believed that energy can't be destroyed and has to go somewhere, the theory of recycled souls has some merit. This theory makes sense to me. I have come across people who I consider "old souls." They seem to be wise and compassionate beyond the average person. They seem to have gone through this whole life process a multitude of times and are nearing the end of their growth process. I think of them as "old souls." And then I have also come across people who seem to be brand-spanking-new souls who have an awful lot to learn.

*"Now about those ghosts. I'm sure they're here and I'm not half so alarmed at meeting up with any of them as I am at having to meet the live nuts I have to see every day."*
*—Harry S Truman*

# Book Two: TMI

# There's No Such Thing As TMI

Ok…I don't know who came up with the term "TMI," as in "Too Much Information." I believe in too much information in terms of the Internet and the ton of garbage that can be found therein, but in terms of human beings communicating with each other…there is no such thing as "TMI".

I will never understand the stigma attached to talking about menstrual cycles, hemorrhoids, sex, wedgies, stretch marks, constipation and every other topic that makes most folks cringe. I remember back to my early teens when my body was changing and my hormones were in an uproar. I felt so alone. No one talked to me about *anything.* Don't get me wrong. I love my parents and I think they did a pretty darn good job as parents go because I am fairly well-adjusted (unless you consider this book the babblings of a deranged person) and I am—for the most part—very happy with my life and how things have turned out. Considering I am divorced with four children, one of which has a tattoo of a guy with horns on his back, drive a '98 white minivan with 150,000 miles on it and a ding running down the entire length of the driver side, am stretch-marked from breast to ankle from becoming quite large during four pregnancies, and average $5.00 in my checking account, continuing to be a perpetually perky person is really saying something! But, I digress.

## Sex

I wish my parents had been a little more open about things. I would have benefited from someone explaining to me just exactly *what* a penis looked like and exactly *how* it was going to fit when the time came. My father was a total prude and very careful about never being caught so I never got the mentally-scarring sneak-peak experience that most kids received. I had the ritual fifth grade health class in which the boys were taken to one room and the girls to another so we could each get our separate, yet similar, sex education. I didn't get it. Maybe I wasn't paying attention—as I often didn't—or they didn't give the information to us in terms that we could fully understand because when the time came that I saw my first penis it was a horrifying experience.

I think I would have preferred some "real life experience" education instead of the sugar-coated, encoded message that was elementary school sex education. I needed a woman to sit down across from me and say "the penis is a big, ugly appendage that the male needs to stick inside you to deposit the seeds that will make a baby grow in you." That I could have understood. The teenage years are so tumultuous as it is that a reality check would have been very helpful. I could also have used some advice like "From the age of 13 to 25 the boy usually doesn't really love you honey…he just wants to practice shooting his seeds" or "sex will suck when you first have it and for about the first twenty years until the guy understands that stimulating a girl's brain is just as important as stimulating her 'private area.'" (I thought about using the term my eight-year-old uses "her pee-pee" but thought the readers may be put off by such vulgarity (giggle…snort).

I could have avoided years of cluelessness about why everyone was running around enjoying sex if someone had explained to me that when it is done right it can be ever so enjoyable. A man and a woman are like a lock and a key. If your partner does not have the correct lock or the correct key, sex is gonna suck. However, the first time the correct key is inserted into the correct lock …the angels sing, the dams break, and all is right with the world. All I can say is I am glad that I didn't *DIE* before unlocking that mystery. I'm not saying that a "good fit" with a partner is all about sex…it's not. The perfect lock and key don't just correlate to the obvious sexual innuendo, but to the spiritual lock and key as well.

## Itches and wedgies

As further evidence of my belief that there is no such thing as TMI when it comes to human communication, I can honestly say that if my armpit itches while you and I are having a conversation I will more than likely pause the conversation to inform you that I have an armpit-itch which requires attention. I can't imagine that I am the sole human being on this planet that has ever had an itch in the pit. Trying to disguise the remedy for said itch would necessitate an awkward shirt adjustment, a quick swipe at the offensive itch while your friend is looking at the large, puffy cloud you just pointed out that supposedly looks like Brad Pitt (actually I am going to change that to Sam Elliot. I know he isn't the obvious choice of hunky leading man to view in the clouds, but he has always been MY choice for Hollywood hottie…I digress again). The point is if it itches…scratch it…'cuz everyone else itches too. Along those same lines one of my biggest beefs in life is underwear. To my knowledge, underwear has not yet been invented that will prevent the eventual creepage into the crack area. Very annoying. This problem is especially tricky when you are wearing tight jeans because you can't get a hold of the errant elastic to draw it back down into place from the *outside* of your jeans. This tricky situation necessitates the hand diving into the jeans in the rear area and hooking your fingernails in the elastic—because the jeans are so tight you have no real room to work—and forcing the elastic back down over the unprotected cheek and out of the forbidden valley. During my younger years when I still conformed to the rules of "TMI," I felt totally alone in the world with this wedgie problem. Now that I have rebelled against the laws of polite society and discuss whatever I want…whenever I want…I have made the amazing discovery that wedgies are fairly commonplace among my fellow man.

I will say that thong underwear has come the closest to curing the wedgie problem. When you wear the extremely thin-string thong underwear it implants itself in your booty-crack and after a few minutes you don't even notice it anymore. But the thong underwear with a wider band in the back can be quite distracting. I tried a pair of the thicker band thong underwear at the urging from a friend who should be a thong salesperson as she promotes them everywhere she goes, as well as promoting the *adorable* menstrual pads that can be purchased to use in coordination with the thong. I had a hysterectomy before trying my first pair of thong underwear so I can't vouch for the little triangle thingies that are supposed to pass for feminine protection. Anyway, I tried the thick-backed thong and it lasted all of five minutes before I was running for the garage to find my pliers. All of this wedgie information should help boost the population at nudist colonies. They *never* have to concern themselves with this prevalent and troubling problem. All they need to worry about is getting the sand wedgies out while sitting on the beach.

## Hemorrhoids

It concerns me deeply that I know how to spell that word…hemorrhoids. First of all, no one should know how to pronounce such a weird word and second of all, ABSOLUTELY no one should know how to spell it. Why do all the disgusting health issues also have icky names to go with them. Someone should have named hemorrhoids itchy-marbles or swell-nuggets. Much more appealing terms to use when discussing the topic with your doctor.

My daughter's dance teacher came up to me one day and very discreetly asked if I had ever had hemorrhoids. I have been her unofficial sounding-board for years when it comes to bodily oddities. She was speaking in hushed tones through barely moving lips. I gave a hearty "oh, yeah, what do you want to know?" She was worried that she had some type of rectal cancer or something and wanted an explanation of what hemorrhoids felt like and what to do about them. I gave a full description of my experience with them and what I described was exactly what she was experiencing. She was so relieved. I, of course, recommended that she be checked to make sure that hemorrhoids were the real issue, but the doctor only gives you so much information. I have never had a doctor tell me to take a nice, soft, blanket to sporting events as the cold, metal bleachers will reek havoc on your irritated bum or if you are going to sit on the cool concrete sidewalk with your children drawing Halloween pictures with sidewalk chalk that your hemorrhoids will go into seizures. Go to the doctor to find out what your problem truly is and then ask a chatty friend or neighbor for the real "low-down."

## Constipation

Here is a word that whomever named the health issue came pretty close to getting it right. I personally think he or she should have named the problem *an*-ticipation instead of *con*-stipation…you know like the song…"*Anticipation….anticipa-a-a—tion is making me wait. It's keepin' me wai-a-a-a-ating.*"

I met a psychologist when I was working at a hair salon years ago. I did not have any talent in the area of beautifying people. I was just the receptionist and bookkeeper for the salon. We had a regular client who was a psychologist. He finished up his appointment one day and came to the front desk to pay. He borrowed my pen…my favorite paperwork pen…the one with the fine point that didn't leave sloppy ink blobs in the little tiny boxes of the graph-like record book. He finished writing his check and pocketed my pen. When I realized he still had my pen I chased him out into the mall and explained that he still had my favorite *finepoint* paperwork pen and his reply was "I bet you've been constipated since the day you were born." My reply was "How did you know?" All my life I have had a constipation problem. During childhood the doctor told my mother to keep me away from cheese, milk, ice cream and anything else that may be contributing to my problem. Now here I am standing in a mall hearing for the first time that my problem didn't have as much to do with my diet as it did with my need to have a fine point pen to put perfect little numbers in the neat little boxes of my nightly paperwork. You see if I had been afraid to discuss my perpetually-bound derriere with a perfect stranger I never would have found out that my uptightness was more to blame than my diet. Incidentally, I have found that the ever-so-wise psychologist was correct. At the age of 38 when I began to learn to relax and enjoy life and gained some confidence in myself, I am no longer constipated. Who'd a thunk it.

## Menstrual cycles

Menstrual cycles are another taboo topic at dinner parties…not so at my house. When I was thirteen and in eighth grade I was the last female at my junior high to NOT have received "my little visitor." During each mortifying gym class roll call, I listened as each girls' name was called. The student would respond with "here" (if she was merely present) or "here-dot" (if she was now a woman and had her period). The dot was meant to let the gym teacher know that that particular student had her period and did not have to shower after gym class. I was the cleanest girl in the eighth grade. I always had to shower.

Finally, that magical day arrived when I became a woman. My period arrived during a slumber party at my house around 4:00 AM. It didn't just arrive…it came in with a bang. I liken that first menstrual period to the scene in *The Godfather* when the guy wakes up with the horse head in his bed. Picture the terror in being a thirteen-year-old-girl waking up with a sleeping bag covered in…ya know… and the feeling that someone was ripping your innards out with salad tongs while someone else was smacking you on the lower back with a sledgehammer. I immediately clutched my abdomen and started to cry. I went to my parents room to awaken my mother. She led me to the bathroom and wordlessly opened the cabinet door where she kept her "little friend" paraphernalia and then exited the bathroom. WHAT! ? That's it! No little talk, no explanation, no comfort! My family did not talk about such things and I could really have used some coddling at that moment.

These childhood traumas have caused me to backlash the other way and become every child's nightmare-mother. There is no topic I don't discuss with my children. I figure if they are old enough to bring the subject up, they are going to get the full explanation. For instance, the time I was peacefully painting my family room and my 14-year-old son was SIX STEPS AWAY in the living room supposedly watching television with a girl who was just a friend. Yeah right. I came upstairs to get a bottle of water and a little bite to eat to find him on the couch and her on her knees in front of him. The horror! No mother should ever be subjected to seeing one of her children in a "compromising position." It is just as scarring as the opposite situation when a child catches her parents. I made her leave and he and I spent the next three hours finishing the paint job on the family room and discussing the "birds and the bees." He was squirming like a worm on a hook. He didn't want to talk to me about it and he *thought* he knew everything there was to know on the subject. I told him I didn't care what he thought he knew or how much he actually knew, we were going to talk about it. As the hours progressed and I tenaciously hung on to the conversation, I found out—and so did he—that he didn't know as much as he thought. Despite the tons of information now being given at the schools, the current youth seem to have somehow found the same secret book of myths and fallacies that my generation had read. When he assured me that he was "not having *real* sex and even if he were he had a one-hundred-percent-surefire-way-to-not-get-a-girl-pregnant method," I knew we were in for a long night. I decided if he was old enough to have a girl on her knees in front of him that he was old enough for some tough talk. I looked him square in the eye and said "if your surefire way is to pull out before you ejaculate…that is where your youngest sister came from." He turned ashen and his chin hit the floor. It may have been a little brutal but I am pretty sure that I got my point across a little clearer than the school had. He is nearly nineteen-years-old now and not a father yet. Hooray!

My children may *think* they despise my need to give full and exhaustive explanations to many issues facing them, but someday I've got some future daughters-in-law and sons-in-law who will appreciate the extra sensitivity to the opposite sex that I have drilled into their brains. You may think you are the only person on the planet with this problem or that issue, but we are all pretty much the same so why can't we talk about everything. Once I decided to shed the heavy, itchy, scratchy, wool blanket of polite society, I felt exhilarated, free, and invigorated…you should try it. Run through your house buck naked when no one is home.

Scratch that itch while discussing your child's homework habits with their teacher. Yank that wedgie out while shopping at the mall. Everyone with their underwear firmly bunched into their derriere' crevice will envy you.

One other comment on the menstrual cycle topic. Tampons. I am probably the only woman in America who has never used a tampon, but really…they are just creepy. I can't imagine walking around all day with a wad of cardboard shoved up inside me. Yuk.

*"To hear many religious people talk,*
*one would think God created the torso, head, legs*
*and arms, but the devil slapped on the genitals."*
*—Don Schrader*

*"Sex is emotion in motion."*
*—Mae West*

# Breasts Equal Power

This is a delicate subject that I will try to address with the utmost of care. I have spent a lifetime in a body with small breasts. It has been a blessing and a curse. During my ever-so-tumultuous early teens it was definitely a curse. Every girl around seemed to be sprouting like miracle-gro for breasts had been invented, but no one had informed me where to get it.

My girlfriends and I performed the usual bonding ritual of exchanging clothing. The only problem was I could not fill out their bikini tops. They could not squeeze into mine. I could not form any cleavage to go with that low-cut sweater and they were spilling out of my sweaters. I resigned myself to wearing my own clothing and watching the other girls ooh and aah over the exchanges of clothing for an evening of fun at the junior high dance.

I had a fabulous nickname given to me by one of my male friends—who is amazingly still a friend of mine—when we were in the sixth grade: fried eggs. Before my mother had agreed to purchase my first training bra I had "fried eggs" that were topped with little nipples poking through my t-shirts. To my huge embarrassment there was no way to disguise the fact that I was apparently only going to develop peaks and no "mountain" for them to perch on. Year after year I waited. Nothing happened.

The upside to the fried egg story—my cup is always half full (even if my bra isn't) and I look for the silver lining in every situation—is I am forty-something and don't sag…it is physically impossible. I am laughing all the way to the bra store that I can pass by without making any purchases and my "girls" are comfortably nestled in a t-shirt or sweater with NO restrictions.

Back to my torturous youth…eventually, I found other things to occupy my time and let the disappointment of only developing "fried eggs" retreat to the recesses of my mind. I solved the ever elusive answer to the bathing suit issue by searching for a swimsuit I liked, heading to the dressing room with the swimsuit in various sizes, and once in the dressing room switching the tops and bottoms on their hangers. Once I got a match that would work (or be somewhat acceptable) I would exit the dressing room and put back everything but the hanger that had my mismatched suit.

Mismatching the top and bottoms was an acceptable solution as long as I was standing up, but I still had one problem. I could only lay on my stomach at the beach or poolside. When I laid on my back my little breasts would turn into nothing but ribs and my suit top would have to stand up on its own. Heaven forbid someone caved in one of my cups with a Frisbee. The Frisbee cave-in would necessitate sitting up to reshape my suit top.

I had a similar experience at my gynecologist. I had been going to the same family doctor for many years. Once womanhood started to set in I felt I needed to sentence my family doctor to sore throats and stitches and leave the feminine exam torture devices to a female gynecologist. The day had arrived for my first exam with my sparkly new gynecologist, Cara. Her first asset was that she was a small woman with hands the size of a six-year-olds. Life is good. Her second asset was she had such an ease about her manner that no topic seemed to feel too embarrassing to talk about.

The consultation and exam were coming along swimmingly. Cara asked me if I did breast self-exams. I admitted that I did not. I told her I didn't really see the point as I was very small. She said that ALL women needed to do them no matter what her size. Cara had me lay back on the exam table and assume the position. Ladies…you know the one…arm over your head, elbow bent. She then opened the front of my gown and said "Wow, you really are nothing but ribs". Thanks doc.

I digress. The subject of this chapter is Breasts equal power, so let's get to it.

At age twenty-two I was expecting my first child. (Yes…I managed to find a man who didn't seem to care that we were the same bra size.) The time finally comes to meet my little bundle of joy. After his birth the nurse asked if I planned on breastfeeding. I had no clue what to do and was intimidated by the whole process due to my breast size, immaturity, and inexperience. I felt that the poor baby (who was born 9 lbs. 4 ozs) could potentially starve to death and decided not to try it.

One week later I woke up with a pounding headache and breasts the size of canteloupes. It took a few weeks for the milk to dry up entirely, but the feeling of power those melons gave me was something I had not anticipated. Now, mind you, I did not get to enjoy the power initially.

I had to wait a few days for the pressure to lessen so I could breathe and function without throbbing pain.

Needless to say, when the time arrived for the birth of my second child I gave the whole breastfeeding issue a little more thought…for the baby's health, of course. I breastfed for a year. I went to the beach that year with my head held high and breasts meeting the world before I did. They were round, firm and full or milk...but who cares, they were round and firm. I was astounded at the difference in treatment. Everywhere I went the service was better. Men AND women seemed to be intimidated by their presence and bowed down into subservience before them. What a feeling of all-consuming and absolute power. I had finally cracked the mystery of gaining power. Big breasts. They are like the tribal symbol for *Chief.* Everyone sees them and knows that this is an important person in the tribe.

I guess I am just a slow learner. Women like Dolly Parton and Pamela Anderson had this mystery solved long ago.

*"Women are always complaining about men's fascination with breasts. But what if men were absolutely indifferent to breasts? What would women do then with these things that serve one function once or twice in a lifetime, and the rest of the time are just in the way?"*
*—Jonathan Carroll*

*"Some people think having large breasts makes a woman stupid. Actually, it's quite the opposite: a woman having large breasts makes men stupid."*
*—Rita Rudner*

# Triple-Play

I am constantly confounded by the criteria used to decide what is suitable for television viewing. How is it decided what is rated R or just unacceptable for regular TV. I admittedly don't watch a lot of television due to my work schedule and the demands of raising four children, although only three still live at home. My oldest son is eighteen and semi-independent (grin with some eye-rolling). Anyway, what I am trying to get at is I am a bit of a self-proclaimed prude. I may be a little backward in my thinking, but in my defense the system of rating television and movies can be confusing.

I enjoy watching the history channel with my kids. Like myself, my kids find fact more interesting than fiction. Real history can have a few risqué facts here and there, items that can bring a pink tinge to your cheeks, but generally informative without being traumatizing.

One Sunday night I am laying in bed watching a fun show called "Snapped" which is about people who have led perfectly normal lives and just all of the sudden SNAP and kill their spouse or something (I do indulge in senseless viewing once in a while). The show ends and before I could even digest the fact that the show is over an older woman pops up on my television screen asking for callers on a sex talk show. My ears perk up and I think this could be entertaining. I am no school girl, but blushed quite often during the next hour. Some may say I could have just turned it off, but like driving past an accident, I couldn't help but rubberneck.

A female caller was first. She wanted the doctor to give her advice on performing oral sex on her male partner. She was a little grossed out by the prospect and was gagged when his "member" was drawn too far into her mouth. The doctor proceeded to pull a pink, rubbery replica of a male member out from her "bag of tricks" and *show* the caller how to perform oral sex by licking and manipulating the head of his penis while using her hand on the shaft. I was shocked but couldn't look away.

It was like watching my grandmother perform oral sex on a pink dildo. (Who has the comet cleanser to scrub that visual out of my brain.) My significant other was peacefully sleeping beside me. I kept looking at the TV and then at him, then at the TV, then at him. He was never going to believe this. I didn't want to disturb him as he needed to get up early so I just kept sitting there with my mouth hanging open, eyes wide, wishing he were awake. At the first movement, grunt, or snort on his part I lunged at him and said "Oh, thank goodness, I am so glad you're awake!". He wasn't really awake initially, but after I launched into a reenactment of the stunning question and subsequent answer, he was fully awake. He is a very patient person which comes in handy sharing life with someone like me.

There were a few uneventful calls in between this initial display and then the REALLY memorable caller. After we giggled our way like middle-schoolers through some other calls, we were both incredibly shocked when another female caller asked the question "I enjoy having three penises in my vagina at the same time. Am I doing any damage to myself?".

WHAT?! If you ask me she has a deeper (no pun intended) burning question than *how* to get three penis's in her vagina but *why*?! I don't think this is a question to be addressed on an educational sex talk show, but one that she may want to discuss with her nearest mental healthcare worker.

I know I am being judgmental and I really do try on a daily basis to not judge others. I constantly try to remind myself that I am not walking in that person's shoes and have no real idea of what they are going through and have no idea how I would behave in their particular circumstances, but sometimes I hear or see things that shock me to the core. The point of all this rambling is not the sex talk, but the fact that this show is on regular television for anyone to see. I can honestly say I enjoyed most of the show. Most of the information that this doctor was giving was informative and important for a responsible sexually-active *adult* to know, however, I think the youth version should be a little more watered-down. I have seen rated R movies that don't go anywhere *near* my idea of too much for my teenagers to see and then I stumble upon a show on regular television that shocks me to silence, which anyone that knows me will say is pretty impossible to do.

# Menopause and Mondo Chin Hair

I would like to know why mother nature feels the need to be so cruel when it comes to aging. One day shortly before my forty-second birthday I was primping and plucking before a date-night with my significant other.

I have one of those little mirrors in which you see a normal reflection on one side and an enlarged reflection on the other. This is an invention that no one needed. Why do we need to see every wrinkle, freckle, and pore in double XL size?! As if it's not hard enough to fool ourselves into thinking we look great (for our age) under the fluorescent lights of a restaurant or bathing suit changing room in a department store, we also have to somehow convince ourselves we still look good (for our age) when staring forlornly into a little mirror, which is also lit all the way around to brighten the horror. This mirror makes every pore on our faces look like a crater on the moon.

Back to the subject; like I said I was primping for a date-night. I was staring into the side of the mirror which gives an enlarged reflection so I could find those nasty little eyebrow hairs that seem to want to stray to the no-man's-land in between the two eyebrows instead of staying in their designated area in each perfectly curved eyebrow.

As I was taking inventory of all of my facial issues I saw something that no woman should ever see; no man should ever see; no child should ever see; a mondo, black hair sticking straight out of my—up to this point—hairless chin. Where did it come from and why did it decide to grow *there*. This hair was about half an inch long and jet black. I don't have black hair. I have brown hair. Even worse, seeing the length of the intrusive and unwelcome hair, I was horrified to realize that I must have been walking around with this gargantuan hair sticking out of my chin for quite some time now, like an angry tarantula waiting to strike. Eeee-gad! I was horrified and fascinated at the same time. I did not immediately pluck it for some reason. I continued to stare at the offensive black hair from every angle and marvel at the sheer *size* of the thing wondering *how* I could not have noticed it up to this point. I think there should be an unwritten rule; if you see a huge black hair growing on your wife, girlfriend, or friend's chin you need to tell her or, at least, pluck it while she is sleeping. When the pain of the pluck wakes her say that you had to slap a spider off her face.

Finally, after about fifteen minutes of staring at this monstrosity I decided it was time for us to part ways. I grabbed a hold of it with my tweezers and yanked. As well as being large and black it was also apparently rooted in my frontal lobe somewhere because I got a sharp pinch in my forehead when it finally released its hold on my chin.

Really, where is the fairness in the aging process? Men lose their hair and it begins growing out their ears. Big deal. Women begin growing beards and moustaches. I feel I can honestly age gracefully with the menopause, wrinkling and sagging to deal with, but I am going to go kicking and screaming into old age if I begin growing black hair all over my body!

*"The key to successful aging is to pay as little attention as possible."*
*—Judith Regan*

*"Thirty-five is when you finally get your head together and your body starts falling apart."*
*—Caryn Leschen*

# Melons Should Be Left in the Produce Section

I have some very progressive opinions and some very prudish opinions. Don't try to find any rhyme or reason to my brain function because I haven't been able to establish any patterns in my forty-two years on this planet, so I don't want you to hurt yourself trying.

Melons, my crude way of discussing breasts and the multitude of other body parts we are inundated with in modern cinema. This rant comes from my best friend calling me and inviting me for "girls night" at the movies. She wanted the two of us to see the *Sex and the City movie.* I watched the show many times and really enjoyed it. I could relate on some level to every one of the main characters. I felt a womanly bond to each one and the dilemmas life would throw at them each week. The show was relevant to me because while the topics were slightly exaggerated for prime time viewing, they were real issues that real women deal with.

I agreed to see the movie with Berta. We purchased our tickets and our totally fattening and nutritionally pointless snacks and settled in for some girls-night-out fun. The movie was excellent. A total "chick flick" that I thoroughly enjoyed. The only little complaint I had was why do so many moviemakers these days feel the need to include everything in the sex scenes except the penis actually penetrating the promised land. Why do they need to be so graphic when they can't come anywhere near my imagination. I have always enjoyed reading because a little movie plays in my head as I am reading. I can visualize or imagine every tiny detail. When I go to see a movie the last thing I really want to see is the actual act. I want to use my imagination. Come on, folks, leave *something* to our imaginations! There was a scene in which Miranda and her estranged husband had decided to make their marriage work and they were having make-up sex. The scene startles you into a deep blush by transitioning from some other scene—where people are fully clothed and doing something other than fornicating—to a full frontal of the character Miranda being boinked from behind. Wow, did I really need to *see* Miranda and her husband in the act or could a few strategic flashes of skin and a few moans and groans have done the trick? I vote for subtle cinema with a little left to the imagination.

Having said my piece about the "nude Miranda" scene, I will say that there is a scene in the movie which used subtle nudity to perfection. Samantha is living in California and salivating over her gorgeously bronzed and toned neighbor who speaks with one of those romantic accents that makes your knees weak. I am smiling to myself as I am writing this in remembrance of the scene…

Sorry, zoned out there for a minute. Anyway, this neighbor is using his outdoor shower and the camera pans down his incredibly gorgeous body from head to shoulders to firmly packed derriere'. It was an artistically beautiful scene because the human body can be very beautiful and artistic depending how it is shown. Then, they had to go and ruin it with another scene of this gorgeous neighbor having sex with two women and once again showing waaaaayyy too much. The romance was gone.

During my early thirties my mom had a friend who read lots of romance novels and then passed them along to my mother. I then read them when my mother was through. Romance novels are called romance novels because they evoke a feeling of romance by using flowery language. The sheer fact that you are *reading* instead of *seeing* allows the romance to remain intact. I think it's time to go back to allowing us to use our imaginations and nix the constant shock-factor scenes in movies. Bring back the romance, artistry and imagination to nudity!

I had a similar experience with a movie called "Good Luck Chuck" with a comedienne named Dane Cook (I think). The movie was cute and funny and really entertaining except for one major scene early in the movie when they show Cook's character having sex with one, then two, then four, then eight, then sixteen—you get the picture—women. They didn't just *elude* to the fact that he was having sex with all of these women…oh no…they needed to *show* you every pornographic part of the sex act except, once again, the actual penis. I am forty-two and covered my eyes! Can't *anything* be left to the imagination? I could have processed the exact same information with a little subtlety. The graphicness is not needed.

The only melons that seemed appropriate in the recent movies I have seen were the huge pair on the blonde dream girl in "The Forty-Year-Old Virgin". The dream scene that this poor sap was having totally called for the frontal nudity of his dream girl. It was funny. It worked. And I noticed that this was an extremely funny movie that had sex scenes—lots and lots of sex scenes because the main premise of this movie was the pathetic guy solving his long overdue virginity problem—and the director of this movie eluded, but did not cram the sex scenes down your throat (no pun intended). Even sans total sex scenes this was a hugely popular and extremely funny movie. The Forty-Year-Old Virgin was a huge hit. I imagine it was bigger than Good Luck Chuck, yet showed much less. Hmmmm. Interesting.

*"My advice to those who think they have to take off their clothes to be a star is, once you're boned, what's left to create the illusion? Let em wonder. I never believed in giving them too much of me."*
*—Mae West*

# Book Three: Instincts

# Bon Apetite'

We, as human beings, feel we are far superior to the animal kingdom. It has always been my belief that all we need to do is look to nature to solve some of the mysteries of human behavior. Our arrogance has separated us from our true nature. We try to fight our instincts believing that our large brain can counteract our basic instincts.

A female bear in the wild will allow a male bear to cozy up in order to get what she needs from him…wink, wink. She then disengages herself from all contact with him and goes about the business of preparing for the arrival of her offspring.

A black widow spider uses her feminine wiles to attract a virile male to take care of business and then she *eats* him. What a novel idea. If only it had been that easy with my ex-husband. The divorce process would have been much less painful if I could have just neatly tucked a lovely red-checkered napkin under my chin, found a large dinner plate, some bar-b-que sauce, cracked a bottle of wine and celebrated the beautiful children we made as I chowed down. This turn of events would be unfortunate for divorce lawyers—and I know a really good one—but would eliminate the need for those agonizing talks with children explaining why mommy and daddy just can't get along. In all seriousness, I wouldn't *really* eat him because I know he is important in the lives of my children, but let a girl have her fantasies.

The subject of monogamy, or should I say, unfaithfulness has been discussed in every hair salon, seedy bar, and Park Avenue restaurant. Why do men cheat? Oops, that was sexist. Why do people cheat? Well, my theory on men straying is that it is just their basic instinct to "spread their seed around." For women it may be a little more complicated, as we are generally more complicated in every area. Here goes…an eighteen-year-old woman sees a virile young man with broad shoulders, full head of hair and smells those pheromones. Her eggs start to quiver and quake. Her instincts tell her that this is a good, strong specimen to procreate with. She starts to sweat and giggle and the next thing you know they are in the back seat of his Mustang. Fast forward ten years. They are now married because they succeeded in fulfilling her instinct to procreate and have created a baby. The male has been slumping on the couch eating chips for many moons. Attention hasn't been sent the way of the wife or kid in a month, and about fifty percent of the full head of hair has now fallen out (and has landed on his beer gut beside the chip bag). The females' instincts take over again and she begins looking for another strong, healthy specimen that will make her eggs quiver and quake since the specimen she currently has no longer resembles an alpha male.

While this theory sounds fairly harsh, if you think about it long and hard you may feel as I do that our instincts can short-circuit what we call our common sense. Our bodies know what we want and need, but our arrogant brains keep getting in the way.

There is one exception to the rule that women need a strong, virile, testosterone-laden male to make her eggs quiver and quake. Men who can sing. There is something extra special that makes a man who can sing very attractive. The proof of this is rock stars. Mick Jagger is not an overly-pretty man, but he can have and—if the media is to be believed—has had some of the most beautiful women in the world. He is thin and pale and prances around like a little girl playing dress up in her room. Without the ability to sing, I can't imagine that he would have been as romantically successful. There are many animal and bird species that put on displays of singing and dancing to attract a female, so, maybe, that is what Mick is doing and he is doing it better than most.

While on the subject of quivering eggs, I guess I will share the little details about a man that can cause quaking on my part—not that you care, but I am going to share anyway.

Obviously, a man with a beautiful head of hair is attractive. I also enjoy a man who is tall with the broad shoulders and slim hips. When it comes to hair, there are places that hair is attractive and places that it just shouldn't be. Hair on the head, a patch of soft, curly hair on the chest, hair on the lower leg and forearm are all nice places to pet some soft fur, but hair on the back, shoulders, derriere', poking out of their ears, and an eyebrow running nonstop across the brow are definite egg-shrivelers in my book.

As well as physical attributes there are other things that make a man sexy in my opinion. A man who is strong in character is very attractive. I turn to mush when I see a man showing love for a child. A man carrying a small child on his shoulders and bringing smiles and giggles to that child's face is priceless. If there are any men reading this pay close attention—women love a man who loves children.

Last on the must-have list for me is a good kisser. This is another hint that men should pay heed to. I remember my first French kiss at the junior high dance when I was thirteen-years-old. I was asked to dance by my first junior high boyfriend. We had been "going out"—which at that age means that you *say* you are going out, but never actually go anywhere together. Back then you just talked incessantly on the phone. There was one phone in the house and it was attached to the wall in the kitchen; no escape. At the dances in my school all the couples preparing to slow dance would converge in the darkest corner of the gym, then hug trying to throw a little rhythm in every now and then. Occasionally, a fellow classmate would stroll through the couples holding a necklace chain over your head. The chain over your head meant you *had* to kiss, just like the glass clinking tradition at weddings. The chain was held over the head of myself and my boyfriend. I had no idea how to French kiss so I let my boyfriend lead. He proceeded to come at me with mouth wide open and tongue thrusting and thrashing like an alligator in a death-roll. When the kiss was over—it seemed like an eternity—I had to nonchalantly try to wipe my face on my sleeve. I was wet and horrified. I left that dance with a solemn promise to myself; I would *never* French kiss again because it was *disgusting*!

The lesson here is a good kiss can make a woman weak in the knees and cause her stomach to flip over; a bad kiss can be a deal-breaker. I broke up with him the next day. Kissing should be slow and tender, not a race to the back of each others' throat ending in an accidental tonsillectomy. Sadly, the boy from my story was and is a wonderfully nice person. My darn issues sent him to the reject pile when he was far from reject pile material. He just needed some work in the kissing department. I guess that's not actually sad for him…just me.

*"A kiss that speaks volumes is seldom a first edition."*
*—Clare Whiting*

# The Mighty Vagina

Any woman who tells you she has never used a smile, a great hair day, or a good-fitting pair of jeans to her advantage is *lying*! Using our feminine wiles may not be right, but it does happen. If most women are honest with themselves they will have to admit that there have been times in their lives when they wanted something or wanted something to happen and felt it was unlikely. That is when they pull their trump card. They sidle up to their husband or boyfriend and turn on the charm. Sex as a trading card sounds slimy and unromantic, but the fact is men become so much more pliable when satiated. Sorry ladies and gentlemen, I didn't make the rules I am just stating the obvious. Don't kill the messenger.

There are some basic facts about men and women that intellectuals want to dismiss. We, as a species, are far too advanced to fall into the trap of being led around by our hormones. Bull-pucky.

As stated before, one of our biggest flaws is tossing our basic instincts out the window and foolishly believing that we are way too intelligent to be ruled by our hormones. One of the most basic of needs is the need to procreate. Most women have that biological clock ticking loudly and screaming things at us like: "must have baby, must pat baby butt, must douse something in baby powder, must dress something up in tiny ruffled clothing, must feed and nurture something." We just can't help it.

We unknowingly use that smile, or great hair day to attract as many strong, vigorous males as possible to then whittle down the possibilities of which one would make the strongest offspring. We *need* to attract in order to assure ourselves we have the strongest candidate for the future of our offspring. How else are we going to broaden our choices and choose the very best possible candidate?

All these years I thought that I was "in love" with the boyfriends I had. Really I just wanted their sperm. Who knew? My chemical make-up was mixing with theirs; If the chemistry clicked a relationship could ensue. No chemistry, no relationship.

On the flip side of that coin is the male biological clock which screams out slightly different urges, but with the same end result. The male clock ticks out something like: "must insert my seed into anything with a sheath, I am mighty and strong and the world should be filled with MY offspring. This assertion may not be *exact* but it runs along those lines.

I honestly have no idea of the actual numbers of men or women being untrue to their marriages or serious relationships. But in my small corner of the world I have witnessed both men and women straying.

Now the purpose for all this meandering about men and women and instincts is the BIG truth that no one ever talks about. The Mighty Vagina.

I know many people will find my assertions distasteful, but before completely dismissing them really chew on them for awhile. Think about your own life and try to be completely honest with yourself. You don't have to admit it to anyone else, but admitting to yourself can be liberating.

The Mighty Vagina gives women a type of power unknown to men. Men can be physically strong, but will never understand the type of power this body part gives a woman.

You see a man in the mall holding his wife's purse as she tries on her one hundredth pair of jeans only to dismiss them as making her butt look big. Do you really think that man is standing there just to be supportive? Is he standing there because he *enjoys* the mall? Is he standing there because he wants to ensure that his wife has chosen the jeans that will best enhance her assets for her well-being and self-esteem? No. That man is standing there enduring the hell on earth that I call the mall because she has what he needs. He hopes that by helping and encouraging her he will get to visit the promised land later.

Now, there is an exception to this rule; gay men. Gay men are immune to the allure of The Mighty Vagina and therefore are an asset to straight men. Every straight man should have a gay male friend to help them decipher whether a woman is marriageable material or even a decent human being. The immunity gay men have allows them to evaluate a woman on all of her other qualities and see her in a true light. While straight men are unknowingly smelling hormones that will eventually turn their brains to mush the gay man is sizing her up and seeing her as she really is.

On a side note, I love the gay men I've met. They are the coolest, most talented human beings I know. I worked at a hair salon years ago and we had one male stylist. His name was David. He was flaming. David wore the best clothes. He had the best hair. He had a slight Spanish accent that he spoke through the most gorgeous full lips you have ever seen. A woman could walk through the front door of the salon with three straggly grey hairs on top of her head and when David was done with her she looked like Pam Anderson on the cover of Playboy. He could make *anyone* look good.

All of the gay men that I have known over my lifetime put me to shame as a woman. They would all make a much better woman than I do. They dress better than I do. I wear bright blue snoopy pajama pants and fuzzy slippers to the grocery store. My socks *never* match (after years of wasted socks because I put pairs into the washer and unmatched pairs come out, I wear the unmatched pairs). They accessorize better than I do. My idea of an accessorized outfit is wearing a bra. They express their feelings better than I do and their homes are decorated better than mine. I am a pathetic excuse for a woman. My hair is never done. I wear makeup on rare occasions when I need to meet one of my children's teachers or go on a job interview. I have a total potty-mouth and my home is comfortable but a decorator would have a COW if they walked through my mismatched, completely thrown-together-as-an-afterthought home. I have a full size basketball hoop in my living room. We can shoot hoops while cooking dinner.

The best way to describe myself is a cross between Candace Bergen's character on Murphy Brown, Roseanne on her show and in real life, and Sandra Bullock's dorky character in Miss Congeniality. Murphy Brown was bitchy and bossy, yet glimpses of softness and femininity would escape every now and then. I have always liked Roseanne and felt she was misunderstood. I didn't know it when I was young, but I am pretty sure I grew up as white-trailer-trash. I always thought Spam was an appropriate main course for any respectable dinner.

Roseanne was bold and brassy, crude and vulgar, but I never got the vibe that she was out to hurt anyone. Sandra Bullock's character in Miss Congeniality cared more about what she was accomplishing than all the trappings and labor it takes to be ultra-feminine. I waver back and forth between days when I want to "feel pretty and feminine" and days when I just throw in the towel and say "being girly is just too damn much work." I paint my nails on occasion (very few occasions) and then turn around and drool through the tool section at the local hardware store.

I truly believe that chemistry is to blame for the masculine and feminine traits we all exhibit. I can't help enjoying the look of a beautiful male body anymore than a gay man can. Gay, straight or in between is chemistry, not choice. I envision a post-and-rail fence that separates men and women. We are all precariously perched on the fence of life during our conception and as the different components of our development come together we are pushed one way or the other. Gay men are given male parts, but are pushed chemically toward the feminine side. They just fall over the fence to being a man, but have feminine qualities. Lesbian women are given feminine body parts, but some male chemicals that push them just over the fence to female. Then you have the mid section of the field where a man or woman is given body parts and chemicals that make the male/female thing pretty conspicuous. And lastly, you have the men who were given waaaaayyyyy too much testosterone and they are pushed really far out into the field of maleness. These would be the knuckle-dragging, beer-guzzling jerks that we should all steer clear of. My best friend coined a term that I think is appropriate in this particular description; immature-hormonal-assininity. On the female side we have the women who were given an overabundance of estrogen and they are pushed really far out into the field of femininity. These women have never touched a hammer, have lifetime subscriptions to all female self-improvement magazines, think "duck" tape is something used to repair injured Mallards and feel men are here to cater to their every whim because if they did anything for themselves they may break a nail.

So, the next time you want to try to change someone remember that some traits are learned and some are just in our chemical and genetic make-up. I am pretty sure I just fell over the fence into the female side of the field. I have enough "sugar and spice and everything nice" to make me a girl, but enjoy a plethora of traditional guy stuff.

After digressing a bit, remember if you're female…use those powers for good and if you're male…be careful how much power you give to The Mighty Vagina.

*"I am a marvelous housekeeper.*
*Every time I leave a man I keep his house."*
*—Zsa Zsa Gabor*

*"A man's wife has more power over him than the state has."*
*—Ralph Waldo Emerson*

*"Man has will, but woman has her way."*
*—Oliver Wendell Holmes*

Thanks Berta, I had a really good time. Can I see you again ?
Suuure, Stud. I'll call you.
STUD
Sucker !

# Did Cavemen Suffer From Depression

There are so many wonderful things that progress has brought us, but I think we pay a hefty price for some of those wonderful things. I am not always sure the wonderful things are worth the price.

I look around at the small community where I live and each and every family seems to be dealing with a problem that progress has wrought. I often wonder if cavemen suffered from things like ADD, anorexia, penile dysfunction, cancer, obesity, or depression.

The group of cave-dwellers I envision are struggling just to find food, so the thought of starving themselves to death is not a wish, but something they are striving *not* to do. We haven't polluted the planet with all our chemicals so cancer is unheard of. And I don't see any cave-men who cannot get or sustain an erection. Only the strongest continue the species so the offspring are the best of the best. I certainly don't see any overweight cave-people as they have to work for every morsel they partake in. ADD is not really an issue because they don't have twenty commercials per half-hour TV episode to short-circuit their brains. They easily focus on one task at a time because that is how their brains have been wired.

Living in a cave, hunting your own food, only the strongest procre-ating all sound like such a severe life but was it really so bad? Life was short and simple. They had problems too but when the problems are mostly life and death issues, I can't imagine there was much time for worrying about other things. Sounds kind of blissful to me.

Along the lines of my imagination, I consider our planet a living thing. I have a lot of respect for this big rock called Earth. Because I think of the Earth as a living thing I imagine how "She" feels about what we are doing. I can't imagine she is happy. I envision her pain when we slice her open and insert lots and lots of garbage causing her cancer, devastate her rain forests thus destroying her air conditioning and causing her heat flashes, pollute her air causing her asthma, and dam up her major water arteries causing poor circulation resulting in stroke or heart attack. If I were her I would have a hearty bowl of bran flakes and a large glass of prune juice in order to evacuate us from her system.

*"The greatness of a nation and its moral progress can be judged by the way its animals are treated."*
*—Mahatma Gandhi*

# World Peace and Warring People

I am not sure if it is reality setting in or I am just becoming more and more jaded the older I get, but I just don't really believe in world peace anymore. In order to achieve world peace we would have to quash some of the most basic instincts in ourselves and our fellow human beings.

Since the first humans were walking around on their knuckles I will just bet there have been skirmishes. Fights over food, fights over mates, fights over territory, and fights just because they looked at each other the wrong way.

We pray for world peace and then turn around and purchase a pay-per-view fight. We sadly shake our heads at the evening news as peoples all over the world are doing horrible things to each other, then, once the news is over, we turn to ESPN and watch two men, or women now, duke it out. We love a good hard hit in an NFL game. We love a good hard slide tackle in a soccer game. And, oh the joy, when that NHL player gets sandwiched between his opponent and the glass; The hockey players then throw down their gloves and sticks to play rock 'em-sock 'em-robots. We love that.

It seems to be a basic fact that humans like conflict and competition. Humans like to hide their eyes to brutality around the world, yet open those same eyes wide to watch WWF wrestlers throwing each other around a cage with blood oozing down their faces.

Very contradictory.

I don't have a clear cut theory on *why* we like to fight so much, but my guess is there was a baser reason for this particular instinct. Possibly "survival of the fittest" comes into play. We just may flex our muscle to show who really should be mating and who really should go sit in the corner of humanity with no seed spreading duties.

Once again, look to nature for enlightenment. Animals fight for the best male or female to mate with; animals fight over territory; and some animals fight just to kill.

How can we expect world peace when we are a basically warring species. We say we don't want war, but United States president's seem to enjoy invigorated popularity when we are on the verge of war and then popularity decline once we get bored and tired of spending money on said war. People seem to treat their neighbors and countrymen a little better and become more patriotic when it is "us against them."

From the time our children are very small we place them in competitions. Soccer, football, and karate to name a few. These are competitions to see who is better, who is stronger, and who the "champion" is; the champion being the strongest and best person or team. Humans love competitions and being declared the best or strongest at something.

What is a war really but a competition to assert your will on someone else. Many a war has been waged over religious beliefs, but the deeper conflict is who is right (or the champion) and the stronger of the two parties is declared right simply because they win.

Don't get me wrong, I would love to live in a world without all the senseless bloodshed and cruelty. It especially disturbs me when children are involved in war, but how can we expect to stop something that is apparently ingrained in us. Be the biggest, brightest, strongest, smartest you can be. Some humans use that competitive spirit to get a degree and launch into a six digit salary while others use that competitive drive to kill the cheerleader competing against their daughter for that coveted spot on the squad. I have been in the business world and it can be pretty cut-throat. You don't generally see a guy in a suit carrying an automatic weapon with which to take out his competition for a job or a client, but the instinct to be "top dog" is strong.

So as depressing as this will sound, I think our search for world peace is sheer folly. Can you recall a time in history…any time…when there was complete peace amongst all peoples on this planet? Why do you think that is?

The last point on this subject is: any time a tenuous peace seems to be made between warring peoples, it seems to only be able to come about through force from an even stronger people. Get it? There is no peace. It is just the will of the strongest being forced upon the weaker. The champion claims their prize. Two groups of people didn't throw down their weapons, shake hands, and admit that all this fighting is silly. Two groups of people were *made* to see the light through force or threats of force. This realization makes me sad, but on some odd level helps me to understand the craziness in this world.

One interesting side note: I am definitely oversimplifying, however, what is up with the Swedish and Canadians? I can't recall a time when they were in the news that much due to warring and bloodshed. Possibly the making of Swedish fish and maple syrup keeps them in perpetually good moods. The Middle East, on the other hand, seems to always be in turmoil. Maybe the Middle Easterns need a trademark sugary-sweet product to lighten their moods.

*"In the end, no amount of American forces*
*can solve the political differences that lie at the*
*heart of somebody else's civil war."*
*—Barack Obama*

*"War – An act of violence whose object is to*
*constrain the enemy, to accomplish our will."*
*—George Washington*

*"Few people can be happy unless they hate*
*some other person, nation, or creed."*
*—Bertrand Russell*

WORLD PEACE RALLY
I propose we stop ALL War!
Wrap it up, Frank. Wrestling is on tonight. Cage match.
Peace Not War
No More Bloodshed
Love One Another

# Children Are Not Born Blank Slates

To think that children are born complete blank slates for us to draw and doodle and mold any which way we like is just silly. They all have very individual styles and personalities. There is something to love about each one of them just as they are.

First up we have my oldest son. He has been stubborn since *before* he was born. He has a good heart that gets lost in all the fabulous schemes his constantly churning imagination can dream up. I was pregnant for a very long time with this one. I know every woman says that, but I really was pregnant way toooooo long.

I was due at the beginning of September and finally by the third week of September I had no signs of launching into labor so the gynecologist decided to induce. There were twenty people in my hospital room pushing and pulling from every direction. Orders were being shouted and pain was the order of the day. Hours I pushed with that boy and he just did not want to come out. Almost twenty years later I can honestly say that not much has changed with him.

He eventually did make his entrance into the world at nine pounds/four ounces. He was bone dry from lack of amniotic fluid that eventually dries up when the baby gets over baked. The boy had two teeth within days of being born. The doctor thought the teeth were already there and we just didn't notice since generally newborns don't have teeth.

He walked early and talked early; painted the television green and doused the living room in talcum powder. He could speak more coherently than most of my friends. By the age of four I had been trying to potty train him for quite a while. He absolutely didn't fall for any of that "honey, don't you want to be a big boy?" stuff. He did not care one bit if "all the other kids were using the potty." He didn't care if the other kids weren't wearing diapers to preschool. He did *not* want to grow up and take any responsibility for cleaning his own backside. He enjoyed having someone else do it for him and did not see any reason why things should change.

He is now nineteen-years-old and going kicking and screaming into adulthood. He doesn't care if all the others kids are going to college or getting jobs and their own apartments. He doesn't want to have to work that hard to take care of himself and he finds no embarrassment in admitting that he *still* does not want to grow up.

He is an enigma because as much as he doesn't want to grow up, he can always be one of the most responsible people I have ever known when help is needed. He was very young when he needed to help with three younger siblings after I had a hysterectomy or was suffering from a particularly nasty bout of the stomach flu. He immediately became this sweet, reliable, responsible young man who took care of everything. As soon as I was back on my feet…he reverted back to his refusal to grow up. Very frustrating, but super-entertaining kid. He has provided me with so many stories for my old age. I could probably write an entire book just about all of his escapades. Trust me, some of them would curl your hair.

Second, we have my next son who could not be more opposite from son number one. He is this quiet, studious, mega-responsible young man. He just turned sixteen-years-old and will voluntarily clean, do laundry or dishes. He is always offering to buy dinner out when no one feels like cooking. He also cooks incredibly well and enjoys watching the food network for new meal ideas. He has always tried to grow up before his time and be responsible for everything on his own. He has been working and saving his own money for years. Upon turning sixteen he was able to purchase a 2005 cherry-red Mustang by himself; what an accomplishment.

I knew from the time he was very young that he was going to be completely different from his older brother. When we took him to a small, local amusement park and put him on the bumper cars he very carefully steered *around* all the other cars. With white-knuckled precision he avoided all crashes and altercations and breathed a sigh of relief when the ride finally stopped.

A prime example of the mellow personality of this boy is that if I asked him if he wanted me to hand him a million dollars his response would be "I gueess so. Maybe. Sort of." If I asked him if he wanted me to give him the black plague his response would be exactly the same. “”I gueesss so. Maybe. Sort of.” It’s like pulling teeth to get a yes or no answer out of him. I need to check for a pulse sometimes just to be sure.

Next, is my third born; my first daughter. She is a combination of the two boys. A daredevil on the odd-numbered days of the month and a studious achiever on the even-days is the best way to describe her. She is comfortable in a glittering costume dancing on a stage one day and in a big, baggy basketball uniform the next. Interestingly enough, she is very much like me, yet not a Gemini. I guess that negates my “Gemini theory” found later in the book.

I recently had to trade in my old minivan which I have had for years. Bessie, as I affectionately called my van, had 155,000 miles on her and she just didn’t want to go anymore. After an exhaustive search of the three used vehicles in my area that I could afford I finally decided on door number three and purchased my new-old vehicle. It was a 10-year-old jeep Cherokee sport with 90,000 miles on it. I was assured by my many friends—that had owned jeeps at one time or another—that a jeep was indestructible. So a jeep it was.

A few days after the purchase of the jeep my daughter and I were riding past the dealership that now had Bessie, my old van. I looked in their back lot and there she sat looking destitute. I felt as if I had abandoned her after all the years of loyal service she had provided. I hauled kids, rocks, mulch, wood, cleaning supplies, soccer tournament equipment…you name it…that van hauled it. My guilt was great. As I was lamenting my abandonment of Bessie, my thirteen-year-old daughter turned to me in a very studious and intellectually-serious sounding voice and said “Mother, the van is an inanimate object.” Well…fine. She is so smart and I am so silly. I didn’t even get a moment to process the intelligent statement that my baby had made and be proud because in the next second she turns to me and says, “Look what I can do. I can touch my tongue to my nose.” Sigh… so much for the intelligence. Just as I was beginning to believe the schools’ analysis of her as “advanced,” she reverted back to being the Lucille Ball of my household. How can you not love a kid who can help you with *your* homework and then make you laugh out loud.

She has been babysitting for a few years for a family up the street with a six-year-old and four-year-old twins. She runs their household like a veteran mother and then comes home and falls *up* the stairs. Her favorite saying after taking a fall (which happens often) is to bounce up quickly and say "I'm OOO-kaaaay."

Last, but certainly not least, is my youngest daughter. (It was nice how the universe sent me two boys and then two girls. Everyone had someone to fight with or play with.) This one is the princess. I firmly believe her true destiny is to grow up and become leader of a small country. The love of a multitude of adoring people, lots and lots of pretty pink clothes, a tiara, and a posse to follow her around and see to her every desire is a life that would suit her just fine. Don't get me wrong. This is not a mean or spoiled child in the conventional sense. She is very sweet and loving. She has a strong need to help and please people. I am sure she would use the power of being a world leader for good purposes.

Her need to be helpful was evident in her assistance with a flower-planting afternoon once when she was about four-years-old. She and I had planned all week to visit a local greenhouse and purchase a flat of flowers. She loves flowers and all things pretty. After our purchase we went home with the flat and began planting. Her job was to pull each plant out of its little plastic cell and hand it to me after I had made a small hole. We worked together like a well-oiled machine. We planted and planted and planted…and planted…and planted. Finally, I said "Wow, there are a lot more flowers in this tray that I thought." I looked up and saw that the tray was empty. Phew, we are done.

I started to gather my tools to put them away in the garage when she handed me another flower. "Where did you get that one from?" She pointed at the other side of the house. She wanted to be helpful and make more flowers and more flowers to plant, so she just kept pulling ones we had already planted out of the ground and handing them to me. We were just planting the same flowers over and over again in new places. Gotta love her.

*"Before I got married I had six theories about bringing up children; now I have six children and no theories."*
*—John Wilmot, Earl of Rochester*

# Book Four:
# Common Sense

# Teenagers

I read an article in National Geographic on the workings of the brain. Among other topics the subject of an incomplete teenage brain and the ability to drive was discussed. We continually put tons of steel in the hands of teenagers. Why? The article stated that the teenage brain has not yet fully developed and the ability to think through decisions is impaired by this incomplete growth. Car rental companies are the only ones that have it right. Some companies will not allow you to rent a car until you are twenty-five. Twenty-five is the approximate age when the brain has completed its growth process (This explains why it is so hard to get good service at the grocery store checkout).

As I contemplate this subject and its basic truth, I am reminded of a few events from my teen years which would appear to corroborate the National Geographic article.

One occurrence that comes to mind was shortly after I received my drivers' license. My father was giving me pointers and safety tips; I gave him the perfunctory blank stare and pretended to be listening. I was actually thinking about who I was going to be socializing with once I extracted myself from "Driving Basics With Dad".

I eventually went into a comatose state and once drool started running down my chin my father gave up on "Driving Basics with Dad" and headed off to polish his tools or something. I called up a few of my friends and I planned our afternoon of merrymaking.

After showering and primping for an hour or so, I left the house and picked up a friend of mine and headed to the local bowling alley. We were meeting up with a few more friends for a thrilling afternoon of playing Ms. Pacman, shooting pool and flirting.

This event was taking place during the winter months. We had just had a snowstorm the day before and one of the topics my father covered during his "driving school" was what to do in case of fishtailing on icy roads. I heard him say something about steering in the opposite direction when you start sliding…or something like that. So…I decided to steer quickly back and forth on an icy road to *make* my car (actually my dad's car) start fishtailing and then would show my superior driving skills by then steering the car *out* of the fishtail and continue on our way. The problem is I did *not* succeed in pulling the car out of the fishtail and the car began spinning in complete three-sixties. Round and round we went banging off the small embankments on each side of the road like the silver ball in a pinball machine. The car eventually landed back-end up on one of the embankments. The back tires were entirely off the ground so we had to get out of the car and hoof-it to a nearby farm to use a telephone (these were the days before cell phones).

After convincing a nice farmer and his wife that we were not ax-murderers we used their telephone to phone, not my parents, but the group of friends we were supposed to be meeting and had them come to pull us out. After the car was pulled out, we proceeded to the bowling alley….out to eat….and had a spectacular day of fun. I knew I would have to face the music sooner or later, so, I chose later.

When my day of fun was over, I drove home and then entered my house to face the judge and jury with fear in my heart. I told my father that it had just happened on my way home and that it was *all his fault* because he told me I should know how to pull my car out of a fishtail. I convinced my mother that *dad* made me do it because he made me feel like I *had* to know how to straighten a car that was fishtailing. The only way to know how to do it was to *practice* it.

My mother actually bought it, mostly because my father had been teaching me to drive every kind of machinery since I was little and my mother used to tell him—all the time—that he was giving me too much responsibility with dangerous equipment. When I was in junior high my father and I used to drive two hours upstate to visit my grandmother and he used to sit in the driver seat and sleep while I sat in the center of the front bench seat pressing the gas with my left foot and steering the car. Hehehe…dad…you never shoulda done that 'cuz now mom's pissed at you and not me…hehehe.

Eventually, my mom yelled at my dad…my dad yelled at me…and the whole thing blew over, but not until my father sucked all the dents out of his car. I had managed to dent *all four* sides of the car. Pretty talented I would say.

Another brilliant teenage moment was when a friend called me to go dirt bike riding with some neighbors of hers. She knew these boys and how to ride a dirt bike. I did not know these boys nor how to ride a dirt bike so, of course, I said "sure."

I told my mother what we planned on doing and she said "no way"...so...I just told her we were doing something *else* and went dirt bike riding anyway. Brilliant.

After arriving at the site of my impending doom, my friend introduced me to her neighbors and each one took turns riding back a trail that ran parallel with railroad tracks. When it came to my turn I was given instructions on how to ride this trail. This was apparently a horse trail and as you were riding back the trail and came across riders on horses you were to pull up beside the railroad tracks and turn off the dirt bike so as not to spook the horses. I was given a quick rundown on how this particular dirt bike was operated—in comparison to all the different kinds of dirt bikes that I had *not* ridden up to this point in life—and was sent on my way. I actually made it halfway back the trail without incident. The bike was large and I had opted to *not* wear a helmet as the guy's helmet was way too big for me (once again, brilliant). About halfway back the trail a group of horseback riders approached and I cordially pulled up against the railroad tracks and turned off the bike. The riders passed me with a nice wave and tip of their sturdy safety helmets—helmets are always a good idea—then I started the bike and hit the gas. Unfortunately, the loose stone running along the railroad tracks caused my back tire to spin and it shot me and the bike up onto the tracks. I panicked and grasped the handles tighter. If you have ever ridden a dirt bike you know that you twist the handles toward yourself to "give 'er the gas." The quick acceleration caused the bike to shoot off at high speed at which point the front tire promptly hit one of the wood railroad ties. Hitting the wooden tie had the unfortunate effect of causing the bike to begin spinning, end over end, with me being thrown around like an unwanted ragdoll. I was spinning with such force that the kids watching said my shoes shot off my feet and went about thirty feet into the air. I landed with a thud—slamming the back of my head on the steel railroad track—in a twisted and mangled heap.

The entire accident happened so fast and the slam of the head to the track fooled me into thinking I was just shaken, not really injured. Everyone came running and scraped me off the tracks. I sat and watched everyone ride for another hour or so then my friend and I left for home. By the time that hour or so had transpired, my head felt like there was a guy using a sledgehammer to try and beat his way out and I could no longer put any weight on my right leg. My knee was swelled to the size of a softball.

Two of the guys went with my friend and I to help me get home. I phoned my parents ahead of time to soften the blow. I said something to the effect of "Mom, I'm fine. I just had a little accident. No big deal. Just warning you before I get there." I arrived home and the two guys had to carry me into the house and my mother blew a gasket. I wound up hospitalized for a little while—nasty head injury—and had to have surgery to repair soft tissue damage in my knee. Good times. Good times.

My decision making was not at its best from about the age of thirteen to twenty-one. Why in the world did *anyone* see fit to put me behind the wheel—or handle bars—of any moving vehicle?!

I also wonder why any parent with a daughter ever allows them to leave the house with a teenage boy. I started school when I had just turned five so I was one of the youngest in my class. Starting kindergarten at five meant I was only fourteen during my entire freshman year in high school. When I was fourteen I felt like I was all grown up…now fourteen seems soooooo young.

In February of my freshman year a seemingly very polite and decent young man—who was a junior and seventeen years old—invited me to the junior prom. I did not know him prior to the prom invitation. He courted me during the two months leading up to the prom. He took me to our local Twin Kiss for banana splits…sat at my house watching TV with me…gave me a kiss here and there whilst coming or going. Not one inappropriate moment during the lead-up to the prom. What a nice guy.

The night of the prom finally arrives. I spend two hours primping and preparing. After the primping was finished I had to pack a small suitcase of casual clothing for the post-prom. The post-prom was when you changed out of the fancy duds and into jeans to play games and dance etc.

I was picked up by my date—to be known from this point forward as "the wolf in sheeps' clothing"—who was driving a borrowed lime-green Mach-1. How cool was that?! We arrived at the venue for the prom. First on the agenda was prom pictures. We stood dutifully in line with all the other spiffed and shined couples awaiting our turn to look like the perfect couple for the camera. After pictures, we found our table which was made up of all of his friends who were mostly popular jocks with their equally gorgeous and popular girlfriends. Everyone at the table was older than I was and much more experienced about dating and what it meant to have an older boyfriend (there really should be a handbook explaining these things…although, my book is kind of like a life handbook…for the maturity-challenged).

We had a lovely dinner and all of the more mature girls were really nice to me and didn't make me feel like the little fourteen-year-old at the table. When dinner ended we sat and chatted at the table for a while and then someone said "Time for the post-prom fun". "Oh goody," I thought. "I heard there will be volleyball. I love volleyball."

We all got up and made our way to our vehicles to get our little suitcases full of casual clothing. I was led to "our room" by my *wolf in sheeps' clothing* so I could change. "What room?" I asked. "Our room for the night," he said. "Why do we need a room if we are going to be dancing and playing volleyball all night?" I queried. He smiled and said that we weren't *really* going to the post-prom. We were going instead to party in each other's hotel rooms all night. Each couple had their own room and we were going to have "grown-up fun," not "hanging at the dorky post-prom."

Huh? I was bummed. I love volleyball.

After what felt like hours and hours of post-prom fun, which amounted to my *wolf in sheeps' clothing* getting totally drunk, I was led back to "our room." Once alone in the room he proceeded to coerce, cajole, push and plead with me to have sex. He tried every line in the book. He explained that we had been dating a really long time, he had invested *two whole months* into this "relationship," had spent a ton of money on the prom tickets, had spent money on flowers for me, had spent money on prom pictures and finally had spent a bundle on "our room." I owed him. Well, I didn't see it that way. I refused to "go with the program" and he eventually got really mad and passed out.

I spent the night being intermittently scared and angry. I was confused because the "gentleman" I was at the prom with was nothing like the sweet, banana-split-eating guy who had been squiring me around for the past two months. What happened? Where did the nice guy go? The next morning he awoke like an angry, starving bear from hibernation, showered and drove me home—in the way-cool lime-green Mach-1—at around 100 miles per hour. We skidded into my driveway at which point he tossed my little suitcase into my front yard. I trudged into the house to a greeting and third-degree from my parents. They wanted to know all the details on how my first prom had turned out. I told them it was fun and left out quite a few details. I sat at our kitchen table having breakfast and reading the Sunday comics from the newspaper. I didn't lose my virginity that night, but I sure lost my innocence. That was a lesson that I never forgot. On a side note, I kind of hope that my Jekyll-and-Hyde prom date is now a father with a daughter about fourteen-years-old and headed for a first prom one of these days. I don't wish any harm to the daughter, but hope at least once in his life he feels the sting of worry over the protection of a daughter.

I was determined to grow up my way and at my pace, but didn't pay enough heed to the fact that sometimes people put their best foot forward during courting and don't let it all hang out until after they have you. They bait the hook and dangle it in front of you. The lure looks all yummy and intriguing…you bite…they reel you in and then once they have you firmly in the net and hauled into the boat they cut you up…eat the good parts…and throw the rest overboard for chum.

Wow…that sounds so harsh.

I am a proponent of living with someone before marrying. I would not have said that during my teen years because I had a fairly conservative Presbyterian upbringing and it didn't really feel like an option. I say I didn't pay heed to my prom lesson because I married quickly during the "bait and reel-in" phase of the relationship. I found out within a few years of marrying that I was a victim of the old "bait and switch." I got pregnant with my first child two months after the wedding. So, four children and seventeen years later I was an empty miserable fish carcass.

My point here is most of us are generally pretty stupid during our teen years and early twenties and there is nothing we can do about it.

Our brains don't catch up to our bodies for quite a while. The only difference is some of us survive our "lost brain years" unscathed and some of us don't.

Now to my theory on why each successive generation seems to be more and more obnoxious. Teenagers can be very obnoxious…just ask my mother, but each generation appears to have less respect than the one before. I grew up during the "don't speak unless spoken to" and "children should be seen and not heard" generation. My father could strike fear in the hearts of young children just by *looking* at them.

My parents lived a tougher life than I did in the respect that they did not have as many opportunities and material things were tougher to come by. Each generation of children grow up into parents who want their children to have more than they did and boy do they! It is a natural urge to want our children to have more opportunities and nicer things than we did, but in the process of loving our children so much, I feel (in my humble opinion) that we are actually making things worse for them. Children are becoming smarter technologically, but have no clue how to change a light bulb. Teenagers are capable of operating vehicles equipped with navigational systems, video systems, audio systems, and computers, yet don't know how to change a tire. Children are shown how to stand up for themselves, which is a good thing, yet show it by threatening to sue a teacher who has hurt their feelings.

Self-respect and self-esteem are built on accomplishment. If mom or dad do everything for little Johnny he grows up enjoying the instant gratification of getting the new toy, but not understanding that five minutes later he no longer feels good inside so another new toy is needed. The new toy is a quick-fix to make little Johnny feel good, but that toy would have been more rewarding if little Johnny had to wait awhile to get it and had to do a little age-appropriate work to earn it. As children we think we don't enjoy working but it helps us grow up into adults who understand what it feels like to work to earn something. Our self-confidence is raised through completion of something difficult.

My most despised memories of working as a kid were when my father uttered those dreaded words "weed the garden." I would wish bodily harm on him and mumble every curse I could think of as I walked as slowly as possible toward the garden behind our garage. The hours of weeding were spent just dreaming of what I *really* wanted to say to my father or *do* to him for raining such horror down on me. What did I ever do to him? Why does he dislike me so much? I would have an imaginary argument with my father—whilst eradicating weeds like Godzilla stomping Japan—explaining all the reasons why what he was doing to me was *entirely* unfair and uncalled for. The worst part was that upon completion of the garden weeding he would just have some other chore for me to do the next day like polish my bicycle that I left out in the rain the week before. How *could* he? *What* kind of *monster* had I been born to? Making me responsible to take care of the bike I had been given…free… and forcing me to slave a Saturday morning away polishing it, was unforgivable. Why couldn't he just get me a new bike since the one I had was no longer perfect? Wouldn't it have been easier to just get the new bike and save himself from my wrath? Apparently he didn't think so. Now at age 40-something, I am so glad he made me do things the hard way or should I say the right way. My appreciation for the material things I have worked for is great and my appreciation for the spiritual things I have worked for is even greater. Not to mention one other side effect: I love weeding the garden! I find the most solace in plunking down beside a patch of garden snarled with unwanted weeds, the sun on my face, a small breeze ruffling my hair, the sound of chickadees and bumblebees in the background, and weeding until the area is neat and orderly again. That is my church, my time to commune with God, Mother Nature, and the Universe and talk out my woes. Ironically, after spending time in nature I no longer feel as if I have any woes.

*"There is nothing wrong with today's teenager*
*that twenty years won't cure."*
*—Author unknown*

*"Common sense is not so common."*
*—Voltaire*

# Eat Some Dirt

I operate a small cleaning business. I just came home from a one time job for a woman who recently had eye surgery and couldn't lift her head for four weeks. She was tempted to allow her husband to do the cleaning whilst she recuperated but thought better of it after he said he would fire up the leaf blower and have the place clean in no time.

We chatted as I cleaned. She told me about her multi-handicapped son who had been born normal, for lack of a better term, but had had a terrible reaction to his pertussis vaccination. Her son was now thirty-five-years-old and needed constant care.

There have been so many wonderful advances in medicine. I don't claim to be an expert in any way, but do have strong feelings on the subject.

We have begun to sanitize and try to protect against everything. This just doesn't seem like a good idea to me. Germs, viruses, and bacteria are everywhere. It seems to me that our best defense is to beef up our immune systems as opposed to trying to KILL everything that could possibly be harmful.

I am certainly happy for the advances that put a stop to diseases like polio. I, however, was not happy at being forced to give my children the vaccination for chicken pox. I tried to expose them as young children to chicken pox, but not one of them actually contracted it. Chicken pox has its risks, but when contracted young it seems to be a nuisance disease more than anything else. Contracting chicken pox as an adult is a different story. Most rash diseases are much worse when they run their course during our adult years. I was told that the chicken pox vaccination didn't even insure that my children would not contract the disease as an adult. Ok…call me crazy… explain to me again why this vaccination is a good idea. The diseases have risks, but so do the vaccinations.

I regularly send my kids outside to eat their daily allowance of dirt, not literally, I just mean that I want them to roll around in Gods' green earth. Our bodies need some germs to fight off or our immune systems will turn on us. I recently read an article about the rise in food allergies amongst children. The basic premise is that the body needs to fight something and when children have not been exposed to enough food varieties and germs their bodies turn on the foods. Dirt is totally underrated. I love the feel of dirt between my fingers as I plant flowers and sometimes I even eat berries right off the vine or fresh picked strawberries without washing the bug poop off...SCANDALOUS!

If you think through it logically...we are just fooling ourselves if we think we are clean and sanitized all the time. A woman comes home from work...she washes her hands then begins preparing dinner. Unless she has sanitized every single cabinet handle, refrigerator door handle, faucet handle, piece of silverware, plate and pan, she picked up more germs the instant she was done washing her hands!

Another interesting thought comes from a friend of mine from the real estate industry. She and I spent many a break discussing debatable topics. One day she told me I should never eat the mints sitting by the cashiers at restaurants as they were tested and found to be slathered in urine from all the folks not washing their hands after using the restroom. These neglectful people then head for the cashier to pay their bills and grab a mint or two for the road thus sharing their urine with the next customer by touching the unpackaged mints. Wow...that's gross. I have never partaken of a free mint since this discussion.

Another rather interesting discussion she and I had was on sex in all its variations. She is a Gemini, like myself, and I haven't come across a Gemini yet who won't talk about *anything*. The same friend told a funny story of being caught in a rather compromising position by her grown son who made a surprise visit from college. The compromising position had something to do with oral gratification being enjoyed by her husband (did you follow that?). Needless to say her son was scarred for life.

A vague thought started evolving in my brain; Ok...she was the one who convinced me to never eat urine-soaked mints from restaurants yet here she was talking openly about practically licking the urine off a toilet seat by performing oral gratification on her husband.

My point here is not to embarrass anyone, but to get you thinking about the fact that we live in a dirty, germy world and we had better wallow in it a little or disinfect ourselves into extinction.

*"The germ theory and vaccination*
*are kept going by commercialism."*
*—Dr. Robert R. Gross*

*"MMR or MR vaccines (Measles, Mumps, Rubella)...have all*
*become more serious since vaccines were introduced."*
*—Richard Barr and Kirsten Limb*

# Men and Women Are Not Created Equal

I try very hard to allow others to have their opinions; I enjoy a good lively debate. It's fun to try and convince someone with a differing opinion to see things my way. It's oooo-kaaaay if they don't see things my way. The joy is in the debate and exchange of information and opinion.

The joy of debate is it makes you think, makes you contemplate another angle or point of view, and hopefully makes you consider ideas outside of your comfort zone, if for no other reason than the mental stimulation. You do not need to agree, but should attempt on some level to try to put yourself in the other persons' shoes to understand where they are coming from and what could possibly make them feel the way they do.

I have heard so many times that men and women should be treated equally; African-Americans and Caucasians should be treated equally. What should really be said is that *human beings* should be treated in the same respectful manner.

Two pieces of pie cut precisely the same are equal. They are *exactly* the same. Men and women are *not* exactly the same. Using the term equal just doesn't work for me. We are both worthy of respect, we are both assets, and we are both deserving of fair and honest treatment, but we are not *identical* or *equal*.

There are some basic facts that fly in the face of the term equal. For instance, at the current time I am not aware of any men who can lactate. As fun as it would be, it is not a common sight to observe a man snuggled on a park bench gently petting the peach fuzz of his offspring's head whilst the baby suckles vigorously on his nipple. How can a man lay claim to the phrase "I am equal to a woman if he can't breastfeed?

I spent a lot of time sitting quietly, humbled by the feeling of a baby stirring in my womb. I grinned at the rhythmic jumps of the little human being with the hiccups. I cringed at the large protruding lump out one side of my body—like something from the movie Alien—when my soon-to-be offspring decided to do a little stretching. I was privileged to experience the joy of being pregnant. Along with parenthood being pregnant was the most rewarding experience of my life. Other than Arnold Schwarzenegger in the movies, I have never seen a pregnant man (and beer guts and indigestion don't count). So again, how can we be the same or equal?

I have a tool box in my garage that says I am just as capable as a man of fixing something. It is chocked full of cool things like hammer, nails, screws, wire-cutters, tape measure and screwdrivers, but I still go to my strong fifteen-year-old son to open the stubborn jar of pickles. They really do seal those suckers too tight. Men are generally, not always, but generally stronger than women. It's not a bad thing it is just a fact. So, how can we be exactly the same or equal if men are usually stronger?

How often do you hear of the scenario of a husband and wife soundly sleeping in their bed when a loud thump or the sound of breaking glass is heard. In this scenario does the husband leap out of bed in his boxer briefs to go investigate or does the wife jump up dressed in her Victoria's Secret babydoll nightie and say "I'll go confront the intruder this time and you can have the next one". I may be completely wrong, but my bet is the man and his boxer briefs are the ones headed out to investigate.

Why can't we put women on a pedestal and worship them for all of the amazing things they can do like give birth, breastfeed, multi-task, organize…I digress…just acknowledge that there are things that women are unique for. In the same token we should put men on a pedestal and worship them for all of their unique qualities like strength, sperm…I can't think of anything else at the moment, but I am *sure* there are more assets that can be claimed by men.

The point is if we put each on a pedestal and worship them for their individual qualities we will be standing eye to eye on our pedestals, but the gold plaques on the front of our pedestals will read very differently. And that is ok. Let's celebrate our differences while standing on level ground.

*"When men and women are able to respect and accept their differences then love has a chance to blossom."*
*—John Gray*

# Ignorance is Bliss

I sometimes feel that less is more when it comes to knowledge. The caveman never had to worry about a retirement plan, where to come up with money for college, contraception, population control, or global warming.

Television, radio, and the Internet have inundated us with information; too much information. We now have to worry about every tiny detail. It seems every single thing we touch, eat, or breathe causes cancer. We have such a multitude of diseases that it is surprising anyone is alive. Arg…I can feel my chest constrict and my brain begin swimming in a pool of worry. Progress is a good thing, so I am told. Is it really? We have made so many scientific strides that we seem to solve one problem and create ten more. The microwave cooks food fast, but when we microwave in plastic the carcinogens seep into our food and can cause cancer. Cooking over an open fire sounds like a better, albeit slower, course of action, plus, you get to continually poke the fire with a stick. Who doesn't enjoy that?

Ignorance really can be bliss sometimes. I don't watch television much and only read small blurbs in the paper a few times a year. Once I know about a problem, I have to worry about it. I am too sensitive a person to know about all the bad news. Mankind is careening toward the cliff of destruction and we are laughing all the way. I wish I could believe that billions of people will all wake up one day and say "Wow, I get it." And begin doing the right thing every day of their lives, however, I don't see that happening. There are just too many of us with too many opinions to make much headway toward solving the problems that this planet is facing. Yuk. That was depressing.

*"The man who read nothing at all is better educated than the man who reads nothing but newspapers."*
*—Thomas Jefferson*

# Computers Are Evil

I blame the decline of our health and well-being on technology. When I was a kid you had no choice of what to do after school. You did your homework, did your chores and then went outside to play with any available kid in the neighborhood. Childhood depression or dieting never entered my mind. I had too much to do and was having too much fun doing it. I remember one boy in my class who was kind of overweight...one boy. Genetics are hard to argue with. Genetics definitely play a major role in the molding of our lives and health, but our environment also contributes. The boy I remember as being overweight had two parents who were both overweight. Genetics had not been kind to them. They had to work harder than the average person to stay at a healthy weight. I am NOT making light of the struggles that the deck of genetic cards can deal each of us. I am addressing the environmental habits that we are inviting into our homes and allowing to disrupt our natural order.

I have a little handheld "hangman" game that I enjoy playing at times when I am in my bathroom doing...uh...stuff. Other than that I try to avoid those cursed things that sap the mind's will to make the body move. I stand in awed and astounded amazement at the fact that a video game was invented that makes you FEEL like you are actually hitting a baseball or playing golf. Here's a novel idea: go hit an ACTUAL ball or step onto a golf green and ACTUALLY do whatever you are pretending to actually do in your living with simulations of the ACTUAL sports gear using your ACTUAL arm...oh forget it. The Internet is one of my most despised nemeses. I use the accursed thing when I absolutely have to like to get information on my kids sports schedules from their schools. No one likes to use actual paper anymore or make any phone calls which would necessitate talking to an actual person, so I have to have the accursed Internet in my house against my better judgment.

I swear if I hear one more newscaster say "how do we protect our kids from predators on the Internet?" I am going to lose my mind. It seems so very simple to me. Don't let them use the Internet. We, as parents, think we are so smart. We think we can stay ahead of the kids and protect them with our parental blocks and protective software. It is an illusion; just like Laura Dern's line to John Hammond in Jurassic Park: "the illusion is that we ever HAD control, John. The dinosaurs are out there and killing the people we love" (or something close to that). We are fooling ourselves by thinking we have control now or EVER had control over what our kids are doing or viewing on the Internet. Unless you are a parent that is sitting right beside your child every second of every day that they are spending time on the computer your kids are seeing and doing things that put them at risk. My teenagers come home from school and tell me of all the funny things kids do or the websites they are viewing at school. School…the one place that every imaginable precaution is more than likely being taken and the kids think it's a joke. They can circumvent the blocks and software like little professional computer hackers because they have all grown up in the generation of the computer. Teenagers are criminals disguised in the guise of an everyday, ordinary cute kid placed on this planet to break down every barrier we have placed in front of them; it is their mission; their purpose. You can't fight their natural instinct. In my opinion, allowing kids to post personal pages on the Internet is hugely risky, yet, perfectly wonderful, decent parents that I know allow it and don't seem to be phased by the danger. It can't happen to their kids. We might as well print our kids picture and personal information in a nice catalogue for the pedophiles and sexual predators.

The Internet has allowed us to order anything from anywhere at any time. Do we really need that much opportunity and that much range in our choices. Do we honestly *need* that much information. When do we have enough? Do we honestly need to know how often people in Australia have fish for dinner? Do we really need to know how many guinea pigs can stand on their head? I have a very finite amount of space in my brain and when I am inundated with needless information, the really important stuff that I need to know is pushed out the other side.

In the 60's women burned their bra's as a symbol of liberation from a male-dominated world. I propose we all unhook our accursed computers and take them to the back yard to meet a friendly sledgehammer. Liberation!

*"Computers make it easier to do a lot of things,*
*but most of the things they make easier to do*
*don't need to be done."*
*—Andy Rooney*

*"Man is the best computer we can put aboard*
*a spacecraft...and the only one that can be*
*mass produced with unskilled labor."*
*—Wernher von Braun*

*"To err is human, but to really*
*foul things up you need a computer."*
*—Paul Ehrlich*

# One Hooker, Please

Prostitution is one of those areas I just don't understand. Why do we spend so much time and energy trying to stamp out prostitution? I think the deviants of the world who are forcing women and children into prostitution are sick individuals. I am not talking about forced prostitution. I am talking about an adult who chooses this profession and an adult who chooses to solicit said professional. Prohibition didn't work because some people like alcohol and will find a way to get it even if it is illegal. The same goes for marijuana and other illegal drugs.

We spend so much time and money trying to stop people from making unhealthy choices. Well, if they really want it you *know* they are going to find a way to get it. And why are we trying so hard to control an adults' behavior. If some guy wants to take a chance on contracting some sexually transmitted disease by soliciting a prostitute then who are we to tell him what to do? If someone says I don't want to sit in an office all day pushing paper for hardly any money…I would rather roll over on my back a few times a day and make a bunch of money…who are we to be "big brother" and tell adults what is best for them. If someone is hurting someone else, absolutely "book 'em," but if it is two consensual adults…who made us their mom? Once again, I may not agree with these behaviors, but history has shown that if someone wants to do something bad enough they will find a way. Shouldn't we spend our law enforcement resources on the people who are running around causing harm to others; stealing, killing, plundering, raping.

What a waste of jail space to lock up a guy who wants to sit in his house playing cards, drinking a beer, and smoking a little marijuana. Who is he hurting? No one. What a waste of jail space to lock up a guy who is lonely and wants to employ the services of a "lady of the evening." Who is he hurting? No one. What a waste of jail space to lock up a woman who chooses to make a living through providing a sexual service. If prostitution was legal we could monitor the health of the "executive fornication assistants" just like a health care industry worker. Who is she/he hurting? No one. And, just imagine the tax revenue that would be brought in if we started allowing people to follow their pursuits legally and taxably? This country would be out of debt in no time at all! What is the worst that would happen if we legalized sex and drugs? Would it cause sex and drugs to run rampant in America? Too late…they already do!

My point is not that I want to run out smoke a joint and find a prostitute. My point is that I don't understand why we don't focus our energies on those doing harm, instead of those who may have some bad habits, but are not hurting anyone. Smoking is a bad habit…we don't jail people for that! Just like smoking, these other things should not be available to children, but an adult should be able to choose how they live their life as long as they aren't hurting someone else. People are not always going to make the choice that is best for them, but it should still be their choice. We can't dictate every move a person makes to save them from themselves. What's next? Making it illegal for overweight people to eat at McDonalds…making it illegal for diabetics to stop at Dunkin Donuts…making it illegal for people to sunbathe because it is bad for their skin…making it illegal for women to date losers and men to date bitchy women? We can't make everyone do the right thing for themselves all the time; if they aren't hurting anyone but themselves isn't it their choice?

Activities such as consuming alcohol, partaking in recreational drugs, sexual activity and many others are talked about incessantly in a negative manner. It seems that everyone is against these activities, yet, many people are *obviously* participating. It's the big two-faced lie. People want to put on the face of propriety to the world and then go home and put on their real face. The face worn behind closed doors. The face that isn't quite so perfect.

The minister who cries "Sin!" while slamming a fist on the pulpit and then gets caught in an affair or DNA testing proves it's his love-child. Knock it off!! The irony is astounding. And the lesson for me in the way our country makes rules is…do what you want, just don't get caught. Many laws are so arbitrary and run contradictory to the actual behavior of so many of our law*makers*. Make up your minds! Alcohol, drugs, and sex are bad or they aren't. Alcohol, drugs, and sex should be legal or the people making the laws should quit doin' 'em!

*"Yes, madam, I am drunk. But in the morning*
*I will be sober and you will still be ugly."*
*—Winston Churchill*

*"Denial ain't just a river in Egypt."*
*—Mark Twain*

*"What Washington needs is adult supervision."*
*—Barack Obama*

# Political Faux Pas

I am not a huge Bill Clinton fan nor do I despise him. I just feel the need to come to his defense on the whole Monica/ oral sex issue. Bill was blasted for having sexual encounters with a young, shapely intern. Really?…is he the first man or woman in history to show some bad judgment when hormones were involved? I read somewhere that scientists found that blood levels of testosterone rose significantly in men who had achieved positions of power or wealth.

Let me first say that I find dishonesty completely irritating and cowardly. It is much easier to lie to someone than to spit out the truth and face the consequences. I have had some experience with important people in my life being dishonest about really pertinent issues and would love to nail a few lying, deceitful tongues to the table, BUT…I also feel that we as a society are so hypocritical. We expect perfection from our leaders, heroes, and idols. We set them up for failure because we expect them to be the super-humans that we can't be.

We are hypocritical in two ways. First we expect our idols to behave *better* than we do and second we pick and choose the history we will relay to our younger generations to suit our needs.

I have successfully completed my twelve years of public schooling and recall a lot of the propaganda that was shoveled our way in reference to our American heroes. I have done some additional reading and watching of documentaries on the same American heroes during my adult years and there are plenty of facts that remain consistent and other facts that were conveniently left out of the public school systems' curriculum.

While I understand that the history books used in public schools can't realistically say that Thomas Jefferson had a second family, or that Martin Luther King and John F. Kennedy were spreading their seed around or that Benjamin Franklin had an illegitimate child; knowing these facts does not make the accomplishments of these great men any less relevant, it only makes them more human. Benjamin Franklin, for example, was one of seventeen children and his education was almost entirely self-taught. What a *huge* accomplishment!

The focus on achievements and complete omission of bad habits allows us all to grow up with unrealistic expectations of our heroes. Shouldn't we look at these great men and women realistically? Look at them through the eyes of a contemporary instead of a starry-eyed groupie? Maybe we would not be so disappointed when they let us down if we would look at them clearly from the beginning. They are only human and thusly subject to the same failures and mistakes the rest of us face.

I am not bringing up the faux pas of these great Americans to sully their good names or make them look bad, I am bringing this up to prove the point that all things written by a human being can be skewed, including the Bible. We should perhaps take it a little easier on someone like Bill Clinton who was unfortunate enough to commit his faux pas in the information age when everyone around the world knows your business in a matter of seconds or be a little tougher on the historical figures who have committed the same types of faux pas and worse… yet all that is taught about them is how incredibly perfect they were. We need to quit being such hypocrites. Written and oral histories are skewed to create and immortalize when a hero is needed or wanted and skewed to ruin a reputation if that is what the writer intends. This is why an independent thinking person is so priceless.

*"How far you go in life depends on your being tender with the young, compassionate with the aged, sympathetic with the striving and tolerant of the weak and strong. Because someday in life you will have been all of these."*
*—George Washington Carver*

*"Nearly all men can stand adversity, but if you want to test a man's character, give him power."*
*—Abraham Lincoln*

# Medication Side Effects

This subject is one that drives me crazy on a daily basis. Hardly a day goes by that most of us do not turn on our "boob-tubes" for at least a half an hour or so. You can't turn around without seeing a commercial for the latest and greatest medications. The instant fixes. The answers to all of our problems.

Arg.

I have spent most of my life trying to avoid medications. I have read enough information on the natural world to understand that there are so many other avenues to pursue before popping a pill. I am not advocating avoiding medical treatment when needed, I am just saying that we, as a society, need to stop looking for the "quick-fix".

We are an impatient people and the prune takes too long to cure the constipation so we down something that will give us faster results. Unfortunately, the side effects may be hot flashes, nausea, increased urge to gamble, increased urge to have unprotected sex, bleeding from the eyes, nose and mouth, loose and watery bowels, fainting, rashes, irritability and depression; I am *slightly* exaggerating, but honestly… does this sound better than constipation?! Sometimes you just have to "work it out" (pun intended). Take a walk, drink a glass of water, or eat a prune. By the way, all of the side effects listed are actual effects that have been stated at the end of medication commercials.

Every day we are inundated with a plethora of new medications when this planet has provided most of what we need already, but we prefer all of our food and medicines in plastic shrink wrap with a shelf life of 50 years. I really don't want my twinkies to have a longer life span than I do.

I am constantly amazed that any medications are sold after the list of possible side effects are quickly stated at the end of the commercial. The side effects usually sound worse than the original problem.

We need to stop trying to do everything fast and just use common sense. Eat better, move a little more, and, at times, slow down a little more. No excuses. We've got it too easy and it shows.

*"You can't fix stupid."*
*—Ron White*

*"If we doctors threw all our medicines into the sea, it would be that much better for our Patients and that much worse for the fishes."*
*—Oliver Wendell Holmes, MD*

# Examine Your Motives

"What are my motives?" is a question I often ask of myself. I have conversations in my head (and out loud) many times throughout each day. Most decisions in life are made due to the baggage that we each carry with us.

When raising children this baggage we carry effects virtually every decision we make. We parent as we were parented. We parent trying to CHANGE the way we were parented. We parent remembering what parents, friends, boyfriends, girlfriends, teachers, and every other human being we have come into contact with had done to us or said to us.

I have four children and have sat at many a sporting event watching perfectly sane people become boisterous and loud. The perfectly coifed bank teller becomes rattled when another child knocks her child over on the basketball court. A suit wearing lawyer starts yelling sarcastic and derogatory comments at the official for making a call or not making a call that is felt to be a grave injustice. What happens to these people? Or should I say what happens to *us*. I have suffered this temporary insanity myself. T.A.A.I., Temporary Athletic Activity Insanity.

Maybe the bank teller was a quiet girl who got pushed around during her formative years and something inside her snaps when she sees her child being pushed. Maybe the lawyer had a bad call tallied against him during the championship game during his freshman year in high school.

The most bothersome situations are the ones of parents yelling mean comments at their *own* self-conscious children during a competitive event. The child didn't jump high enough, isn't being aggressive enough, didn't run fast enough, didn't get that winning point, or in other words, isn't making the parent look good. The child is not giving the parent bragging rights.

The irony of the parent directing nasty calls toward their own child is that generally the parent making the comments is a nonathletic-looking, beer-drinking, can't-run-for-five-feet-without-becoming-winded kind of person, and didn't play sports in school because they weren't either motivated enough or athletic enough. They are living vicariously through the accomplishments of their children and when the said child is not making them look good enough they become belligerent. In the meantime the psyche of that poor kid is becoming battered and beaten.

So many parents claim they want better for their children; that they want their children to be more successful than they were. Examine your motives. Is your need for success from your child because you want them to do well or is it more of a fulfillment of the accolades and accomplishments that you didn't achieve? Is it possible that it is about bragging to family and friends about the amazing accomplishments—which thusly makes you the best parent on the block—or is it purely unselfish motives that drive you.

*"The best vision is insight."*
*—Malcolm Forbes*

# Designer Babies

I have been very fortunate in my life to be fairly healthy and have been able to live a pretty ordinary life. Yes, ordinary can be good. I may feel very differently if I hadn't been one of the lucky *ordinary* people. I do not personally believe in abortion, unless a mother's life is threatened or there are extenuating circumstances beyond our medical capabilities, but would never protest an abortion clinic or tell someone else what they should do with their own body; they have to face themselves in the mirror. I have friends that have had abortions for their own reasons and I do not think any less of them. I believe firmly in each person's right to choose what is best for their life. Violence toward another is never the answer to solving differences of opinion. I will never understand the need of one human being to inflict their opinion on another by bashing them over the head until they agree. There are many outlets for getting one's opinion across and the power of the word is strong. Look how many people Martin Luther King affected with his words. We all have the ability to get our point across without threatening harm if others do not agree with us. Once we all realize that we each have the right to free speech, but that freedom of speech does not guarantee that what we have to say is right or that others will agree. What we really have the right to do is agree to disagree.

But…now to the subject at hand.

Babies…don't most of us just love babies. Why not? They are cute, smell good most of the time, and do the most adorable things. We females have this indescribable urge to have and care for babies; our maternal instinct. What I don't understand is the science of helping us create designer babies, test tube babies, and multiple births through invitro fertilization.

My heart bleeds for any man or woman who longs for a baby and can't have one naturally. I have to honestly say that my children are the light of my life. I would be lost without them and wish that kind of happiness on anyone who wants it, but I think we are going about helping infertile couples in the wrong way.

There are so many children in need of homes, beautiful babies around the world who need love and devotion. I always recall the scene in *Jurassic Park* when Jeff Goldblum's character is trying to explain to the group around the dinner table why creating dinosaurs is not a good idea. Just because science has the capability does not mean that they should. He says something to the effect of dinosaurs were selected for extinction by nature and we should not mess with Mother Nature. I reference the movie Jurassic Park so much because that particular movie relays an idea similar to how I feel about so much of our scientific "advances." I feel the same way about the engineering of babies. We are messing with the natural order of things. All of the articles I've read or news stories I've seen on the work scientists are doing to pick a baby's eye color or hair color or sex just really frightens me. What if everyone wants a boy first? Or everyone wants a blue-eyed blonde? In thirty years we will have a beach full of blue-eyed blonde boys who are beat red because a lot of fair-skinned blondes burn easily and they all have no girls in bikinis to look at or talk to because everyone wanted boys the decade they were born. Aren't we altering things we just should not be tampering with?

Invitro-fertilization also scares me. A doctor implants so many viable embryos into a healthy female in the hopes that one will "take." Sometimes one healthy baby has been made. Sometimes two or more healthy babies have been created and sometimes five, six, seven, or eight babies have been created. I completely understand the resistance to aborting some so that the others can have more of a chance at survival. I had a situation during one of my pregnancies that brought the topic of abortion to the forefront of my life and it was a very confusing and frightening time. I had been in a pretty severe car accident and was still in rehab to regain full use of my left leg. It had been nine months since the car accident. I had broken my left knee cap, my right wrist, and herniated a disc in my neck. The herniated disc was not initially found and my doctors continued doing tests throughout the nine months to try to find out where the constant pain in my right shoulder blade area was coming from. It was continual and debilitating. Finally in January of 1994 my doctor ordered a nuclear bone scan that should show any hidden fractures or bone issues. A pregnancy test was done prior to the bone scan; it was negative. I would find out later I was actually a few days pregnant at the time of the bone scan. My bloodstream was injected with nuclear dye. I started to have heavy bleeding and cramping. The doctor, as well as other important people in my life, told me I may want to abort the pregnancy. I could not. I have a beautiful thirteen-year-old daughter now. She is a complete joy. I can't imagine my life without her. So, after digressing a bit here, the point is I completely understand the agony of having a life growing inside of you and people telling you that you should end it.

The difficulty in choosing to abort is that if doctors didn't implant so many embryos into the mother, the necessity of ending a created life would disappear. It is like reducing a life to nothing more than a toy for us to play with. Let's buy ten rubber balls so if we break a few we still have more. These are real live human beings that have been created and treating them like a material item flies in the face of human decency.

The other problem with these multiple births is that the human female body doesn't seem to be designed to carry a *litter* of babies. Our bodies seem to react best with one or two.

I've watched documentaries on some of these multiple births and often times some or all of the children have residual health issues. Generally, these children are born very prematurely due to lack of space in their cramped quarters and the mother's body is just too overburdened. They will have to deal with these health issues for the rest of their lives. It doesn't make them less special or not beautiful and wonderful, but is it fair to do that to these children for our own selfish wants? We want what we want no matter the consequences to the babies and their futures. We human beings are so strong-willed about what we want and are smart enough to make it happen…but should we.

Nature is such a wonderful thing. Why can't we just let nature surprise us. Building Babies…doesn't just this phrase fly in the face of Christianity? Doesn't *God* build the babies and decide who should have babies and what babies they get? Do you see any contradictory behavior in going to church on Sunday and praising God and placing your life in his hands, yet visiting a doctor on Tuesday that will help you *build a baby*?

*"Every man must decide whether he will walk in the light of creative altruism or the darkness of destructive selfishness."*
*—Martin Luther King, Jr.*

# Racism

Racism has long been perplexing to me. I just don't get it. What in the world could possibly cause one man or woman to think just because of the color of their eyes or the shade of their skin they are a better or more worthy human being?

I, myself, am Irish. I have a great sense of humor and enjoy a good Irish joke as much as the next person because I take them for what they are; jokes. I don't believe because I am Irish I have to be an alcoholic, but, for the sake of a good joke and not taking myself too seriously I accept that perception about Irishness. It makes a good joke…not a good fact…a good joke. Who cares?!

For lack of a more detailed description, I am female, white, five foot six inches tall, brown haired, brown eyed with a few freckles here and there. Actually, I do have one admission; I am really grey-haired, but Loreal helps me continue to call myself brown-haired. I am extremely average. Average can be a good thing or a curse depending on how you look at it. I am perpetually positive so I think of average as good. Average means you can blend into society fairly easily and avoid some of the problems caused by standing out. On the opposite side average means it is difficult to stand out when you actually *want* to.

I have an uncle who really enjoys the whole genealogy thing and researched our family roots. He shared some of what he learned and a quick synopsis of what he told me was that we were the worst of the worst in Ireland. We were *thrown out* during the potato famine. We were so horrible that when our country was in one of its toughest times in history we were lower than *that*!

Having admitted that the blood of the lowliest dregs of Irish society flows in my veins, I don't feel I have the right to judge anyone else. How can I say that an African-American or Hispanic-American citizen is somehow less worthy than I am? I am a dreg, after all! What do I have to toot my horn about?

Actually, I have lots of characteristics that I enjoy tooting my horn about. I think I am a decent enough person, I try to live my life treating other people the way I want to be treated, I don't abuse my elderly parents, I don't abuse my children, I try to help others less fortunate and I try to be as respectful as I can to our planet. So, being a dreg of Irish society has not doomed me to a life of drinking and crime, yet I still enjoy a good Irish joke.

Now that I've tooted my horn I will state some of my flaws and yes, there are many. I am totally ADD. I have the attention span of a gnat. I can be distracted in the blink of an eye. I talk too much and talk too loud. I ramble on incessantly when I have no idea if my listener has any interest in what I am saying (thus the book).

Actually, I have to stop here and say, the whole reason I decided to put my incessant ramblings into book form can be blamed on two people. One, my best friend, Berta, who has listened to me ramble for twenty-five years and continually says she likes it. She has convinced me that my rambling is a good thing, so she can be partially blamed for this book. The second conspirator to infect you with my ramblings is Kenny Mayne of ESPN. He, of course, has no idea he inspired me in any way but you can blame him just the same. I have a cleaning business, am totally an anal-neat-freak and clean residential homes and commercial businesses during the day and weekends. At night I type and code manuscripts for a company near my home town. One of the manuscripts I worked on was a book by Kenny Mayne called *An Incomplete and Inaccurate History of Sport*. He rambled on in a totally ADD fashion about sports and his life. I really didn't learn anything from the book but enjoyed his humor and wit. I felt connected to this total stranger by the thread of incessant and scrambled thought processes and rambling.

OK, back to the subject. My point in stating some of my assets and some of my liabilities is that we all have both. There is no perfect human being and there is no inferior human being.

I love to watch sports. I spent one Thanksgiving with my family and an elderly friend of my families who spent much of the lovely Thanksgiving afternoon bashing African-Americans and Hispanics. The family friend who is one of the nicest people (if you are his friend) continually used terms like "nigger" and "spic." I wanted to stuff my children's ears with cotton. What I found so ironic was we were watching the traditional Thanksgiving day NFL football game. He was cheering just like everyone else when a good play was made. He was sitting there being entertained by amazing athletes, many of which were African-American, yet had the nerve to somehow imply they were inferior to white people. WHAT!?!? My brain was swimming with the contradictory theme. The family friend has never done anything outstanding. He has never done anything really horrible either, but he is not one of those memorable people who will have a legacy live on much longer than he does. Where is the off switch? Where is the button I can push to make this man realize that he is no better or worse than those "niggers" or "spics" he is complaining about? What has he done in his life to make him believe that he is superior? The answer is nothing. How does one convince someone like that (without offending) that they are ....well...DEMENTED!

Now, having said all that, I am probably going to stick bees in a few bonnets by stating some stereotypes I have noticed. Forgive me the stereotypes. I am not going to use the term "all" at any point. I am only going to use the terms "opinion" and "in my experience." And I am only stating the stereotypes I have seen in my experience to prove a point.

Most of the racism I have experienced comes from the white population and is addressed to everyone else. The reason for this is I am a part of the white population (I use the term white loosely as we are really many shades of tan or off-white). This racism directed at other races has always confused me as "in my opinion" the African-Americans may have a slight edge on us "honkies" in the athletic department and the rhythm department. Have you ever seen a white man dance? "In my opinion" the Hispanic race may have a slight edge on us in the passion department. I have seen very few white women as passionate as Hispanic women. Maybe the extra passion comes from the more temperate climate in the Southern Hemisphere. And, last, the Asian race may have a slight edge on us in the inventiveness category. I know when I go shopping I see an awful lot of labels that say "Made in China."

I know some people are going to get all up in arms and think I am doing some reverse racism and bashing my own relatives. I'm not. I love my family and my history. I just want more people to stop and think about superiority and the fact that there is just no point to it.

If you want to take this one step further; if you are a Christian we are *all* family. We all descended from Adam and Eve. So, if you are going to church on Sunday and proclaiming your Christian-like ways, kindly refrain from bashing all the "inferior people and races" the rest of the week because you are simply insulting your own family.

*"Doing an injury puts you below your enemy; revenging one makes you but even with him; forgiving it sets you above him."*
*—Benjamin Franklin*

*"I always distrust people who know so much about what God wants them to do to their fellows."*
*—Susan B. Anthony*

*"Whenever I hear any one arguing for slavery I feel a strong impulse to see it tried on him personally."*
*—Abraham Lincoln*

# Mommy or Grandma?

I have long felt that the small societies around the world that have their young people do the reproducing and the grandparents do the child-rearing are on to something. When I had my first son I was twenty-three years old. What an immature idiot I was at that age (I'm still an idiot at this age, but who's counting). I didn't know diddly about raising children. I was still very immature and selfish.

We are required to study a book to get an education in the career of our choice. We are required to study a book to learn how to get a driver's license. We are required to get some on-the-job training in most cases before being left to go off on our own.

Where is the training manual or required parenting education before we can reproduce? During our teens and twenties our bodies are healthy and at their best point for producing healthy offspring. The only problem with reproducing at this age is we are STUPID! We are still in the phase of thinking we know everything and our parents don't know anything. Therefore, we don't watch and learn from them. We rebel against them and their way of doing things.

There is the possibility that I am just a really immature person and it took me a lot longer than others to reach the point of realizing that my parents were not stupid. I now feel striving to be more like them is a good thing.

In my case I feel sorry for my oldest son. He was the test subject. He had to suffer through all of my inept and often confused parenting ideas. Starting out as an enthusiastic young mother I read all the parent magazines and listened to all the advice I could get. The result of all of this "help" was that I couldn't define my *own* thoughts and attempt to follow my own instincts. I often waffled on issues because one news report said do it *this* way and another magazine article said do it *that* way.

What I should have done was turn my beautiful children over to my awesome parents to raise, watched and learned, then when my children were grown I could then raise *their* children. My oldest three children (I have four) often asked me why the youngest doesn't get in as much trouble or I don't get as upset about things. They think she is just spoiled. What they don't realize is that I am just more patient now then I was twenty years ago.

My mother appears to me to be this calm, patient, unflappable person. What I don't remember is she was not this calm, patient, and unflappable when I and my brothers were little. It's a good thing that babies don't have much of a memory. Now my oldest son asks me how I can stay so calm during crisis situations. Time and experience.

Generally young parents are not experienced or wise. They have a lot of learning to do and raising children is one of the most important careers anyone can choose to embark on. Parents are influencing the next generation of adults which in turn influences the world. What an awesome responsibility given to someone wearing a t-shirt that says "Your mama was a hamster and your father smelt of elderberries"? (This is an actual t-shirt in my household worn by one of my teenage sons).

*"Having children makes you no more a parent than having a piano makes you a pianist."*
*—Michael Levine*

# Funerals and Diamond Rings; Show How Much You Care

This is a topic that I find particularly disturbing. We need to grow backbones, quiet the noise around us and make decisions for ourselves. Don't determine whether you are a good person by listening to a sales pitch.

I have already informed my entire family and any friend who cares to listen that when I die, I want to be cremated and sent back from whence I came. I do not want a satin-lined coffin made of the nicest wood available. I do not want that gorgeous coffin ensconced inside a titanium-steel, hermetically-sealed crypt of any kind. I do not want said coffin inside a cement crypt with a ten foot high angel standing over me. And I do not want said crypt then shoved into the ground to suck up space on the surface of this planet. There is a finite amount of surface space and each one of us who chooses to be elaborately memorialized is taking precious space that a nice tree or gopher could claim. In other words, a space that some *live* thing could use.

Why would anyone want to go to that trouble anyway? It doesn't matter whether you believe in the afterlife or not or whether you believe that the spirit lives on in some form or not or if you think we die and are just dead…nothing more…finito. Think about it; in all cases the bottom line is the physical body is finished. What happens to the spirit is the debatable subject, but we ALL seem to agree on one thing; the fate of the spirit is arguable, but the fate of the body is definitely… very defined. When you *dead*…you *dead*. The physical body has no further purpose and, like the empty eggshell from your morning scrambled eggs, should be discarded in a useful way. I haven't quite figured out what all the uses for grandma are, but I know if I thought long and hard about it, I could come up with some. I just want to be cremated and strewn about my wildflower garden.

Even if you believe, like the ancient Egyptians, that you need to preserve the body for use in the afterlife, I would still want to be cremated and forget using my body. Or just give me a new model and I will start over with all that walking, talking and motor skill acquisition. I would prefer to be a free-flowing entity as opposed to jumping back into a crumbly, pickled body with skin like shriveled newspaper and no nose because it fell off during transit. Have you ever watched the Discovery channel and seen what those mummies look like? They ain't pretty. Would you really want to reinsert your spirit into a body that will crumble and fall apart at the least little bit of movement? Forget dancing, you would have no toes or probably feet left after trying to participate in a kick-line and imagine the can-can. You do a rousing rendition of the can-can only to have your butt fly off at the pinnacle of the dance when you turn around and lift your skirt. Euuuwwww. Just not a pretty mental picture.

As if dancing in that fragile body doesn't sound bad enough…think about sex. I don't think I need to say any more.

Another good argument against wasting your time and money on body preservation is it won't do you any good anyway. My brilliant and beautiful *almost* step daughter is in nursing school and said that bacteria is sealed up with everyone no matter how thorough the embalming and burial ritual. So if you are sealing the bacteria in…what is the point of doing all the sealing. You are going to rot no matter what, so just skip the mega-box burial and go straight back to ashes.

Now to the real point of this topic. As a child and as a young adult, I sat through the making of funeral arrangements for my brother who died of cancer when I was in fourth grade and my grandmother who passed away when I was in my late twenties. The funeral directors in both instances tried to push my father, who was the central character in both scenarios, into spending a lot of money to show his respect and show how much he loved these people. Bull-puckey. How on God's green earth does spending a ton of money to put an empty shell into the ground show respect and love. I personally think it shows stupidity. Your loved one lives on in your memory and your heart. They live on in the way you live your life because they were an integral part of making you the person you are. They do NOT live on by putting them in a really nice box in the ground.

Just try to imagine what the planet will look like in a few years with a mega-billion population sitting on it right now. If every single person exercised their right to a "proper" burial there will eventually be no surface space left, except for possibly at the north and south pole. I guess that sounds reasonable...let's all have a "proper" burial and then future generations can have the left over space at the north and south pole. Actually, I guess at the rate we are destroying the planet we won't need to worry about proper burials or livable space on the planet because we are all gonna fry anyway.

Along with the amount spent on a funeral being correlated to how much love and respect you are showing...I get very irritated when I hear women talk about the size and type of diamond engagement ring they want.

I guess I am a little old-fashioned when it comes to the subject of gift-giving. I think a gift is something that someone sees or decides to shop for because they *want* to give that *particular* gift to a *particular* person. To me, it spoils the joy of gift-giving when the recipient *tells* you ahead of time that they want this or that, in this color or that color, in this brand or that brand, in this price range or that price range. The worst part is then you have to bring home the "gift" and wrap it up beautifully to present it to the recipient who knows *exactly* what is under the beautiful wrap job. What a vicious circle! Stop the madness! Just say no to gift-demanding! Do not allow someone to dictate what you will give them and how much you will spend. That *completely* defeats the purpose of a gift. A gift is something that reminds you of someone or something that you *want* to give someone because you care.

The opposite of gift-demanding is gift-giving-laziness. This comes from someone who lacks the imagination to come up with a gift idea and they ask for ideas. If you fall into this category, my best advice would be save yourself the trouble and just give someone money so they can go get what they want, where they want, and wrap it up the way they want. Having said that, I don't even think you should bother giving them any money either. If gift-giving isn't a joy, then just don't do it. Christmas has become such a farce and has given many people a sense of redundancy and drudgery. No joy...no joy at all. What idiot changed Christmas from a time of religious rejoicing into a big green and red holiday where everyone has to run around like a chicken with their head cut off.

The biggest gift-giving event that drives me crazy is engagement rings. I was listening to a radio show where a man wanted to surprise his hopefully-soon-to-be fiance' by having the radio station call her and he would propose on air. This gentleman said hello to her and proceeded to pour out his heart on air with family, friends, and tons of strangers listening to how much he cared for this woman and hoped she would agree to become his wife. This beeeeaaaatttccchhh, without one kind word to the poor guy, proceeded to blast him for doing the proposal all wrong. She wanted romance and candles. She wanted the proposal done *her* way. She wanted to see a huge diamond ring to go with the proposal.

I did not know the guy or the unbelievably nasty and insensitive woman he decided was the love of his life, but if I were him I would have hung up that phone and run in the other direction as fast as my feet would take me. That absolute witch-of-a-woman should have been completely ashamed of herself. She not only did not deserve that guy, but I am not sure if *any one* deserved to spend the rest of their lives trying to please a selfish, self-centered person like her.

It is rumored that the first engagement rituals come from prehistoric man. Supposedly, a male tied the arms together and the feet together of his intended wife. He eventually untied her feet. If she didn't run away he would also untie her hands. A piece of cord was left tied around a finger with an end left trailing. Later, the Egyptians and Romans used rings on the third finger of the left hand because the vein in that finger led straight to the heart. No matter where the ritual comes from it seems firmly ensconced in our society so that is what we have to work with. I just don't get how it has become the ritual of a woman going and finding a huge rock that she wants to sport on her ring finger in order to make all her friends green with envy. You know darn well that if there was no one around to see the diamond ring, there would be no reason for it to be so large or elaborate. It's all about showing off. So…making the man you plan on spending the rest of your life with float a massive loan to put a ring on your finger is in essence shooting yourself in the foot. The day after you get married you will supposedly be "in it together" and his debt will be your debt. If the only purpose for the ring is for him to present a gift to you in order to prove his love and commitment…why does it matter what the gift looks like. Shouldn't it be *his* choosing since it is *his* gift to her?

"Happiness can't be sustained by anything externally; it comes from within." I wish I could remember where I read or heard this quote. I believe this sentiment wholeheartedly. So many of us in today's society look for happiness in owning something (or someone) and wonder why the high doesn't last. We wonder around in search of the next thing or person that will make us happy. If I only had those shoes, car, or man/woman as mine…then I would be happy. I just don't think it works that way.

In reference to the guy who was blasted on the radio for doing the proposal all wrong…he should realize that the huge diamond ring or properly done proposal will not keep his bride-to-be happy for long. It is a drug that will only give her a temporary high. When she demands the next thing be bought or done, he will need to snap to attention and pony up to her demand or she will not be a happy camper. He needs to ask himself if he wants to spend the rest of his life trying to keep an unreasonable and selfish person happy.

If a tree falls in the forest and no one is around to hear it, does it make a sound? If a huge diamond ring is put on a selfish woman's hand and no one is around to envy it, will it still bring her joy? I doooon't thiiiink soooooo.

*"People who are wrapped up in themselves*
*make small packages."*
*—Benjamin Franklin*

# Book Five: Completely Pointless Rambling

# My Nemesis

It's hard for me to narrow down the things that irritate me, but this subject holds special irritation value. If I hear the word *fundraiser* one more time, I honestly think my brain is going to melt and slide out my ears like a California mudslide. I sometimes dream of moving to a remote island to spend the rest of my days just to avoid fundraisers.

I have four children. Those four children are involved in many activities because I think it's good for them. I would rather see them playing tennis, soccer, basketball or dancing than milling around on the corner in town. Sports are about so much more than just winning or losing at something. Exercise is good for the body *and* the mind. Being involved in organized activities can help children gain socialization skills, leadership skills and responsibility; all things that will be helpful later in life.

But, enough with the fundraising! I counted one year—just out of curiosity—how many fundraiser packets crossed my desk. The year I counted was a slow year because my oldest son was now out on his own. There were eighteen fundraisers that I can recall. That comes to more than one a month. If I went around harassing my family and friends more than once a month to give money for the activities my children are involved in, my family and friends would stop answering the door or phone when they knew it was us. Also, my conscience would not allow me to make everyone else responsible to pay for the choices my family makes. I don't do fundraisers. I pay for the choices we make and if we can't afford it…they don't do it. It is not a bad thing for children to understand financial limitations. My children don't seem to have a problem understanding financial limitations; the adults organizing all of these fundraisers are the ones that seem to have the problem understanding financial limitations.

In my home, if we can't afford something we don't buy it. Whatever happened to the word budget? Are there no Americans left who know how to live within their means? We don't need to raise more funds; we need to stop spending money!

My sixteen-year-old son has been bringing home fundraisers since his freshman year in high school so that his class will be able to afford a senior prom. You've got to be kidding me. If the prom is that expensive, then someone needs to rethink the amount spent per student to organize the prom.

I pay school taxes so our children can have a public school to get an education. The school sends home at least two fundraisers a year. Stop it! These fundraisers aren't for books or building upkeep…they are for field trips and parties and assemblies. Field trips, parties, and assemblies are fun, but not necessary. I had a great time in school during my childhood years. You went to school…you learned some…you played with your friends at recess some…you got in trouble throwing erasers once in a while…and you went on a field trip once a year or so (which your parents paid for). If your parents couldn't afford to send you on the field trip, then those students deserved to fundraise or get some help. There are definitely circumstances when a child should receive help if the family can't afford an educational experience, but every organization in our hometown has gone overboard with what they feel are *needs* and *necessities* as opposed to *wants.*

Aren't our tax dollars supposed to make all extra-curricular activities available to all students in school. Shouldn't these activities be available to all students at no cost because it is a part of our school system? It doesn't work that way anymore. I received a set of flyers for one of my children's school sports. Mortification set in when I realized that these flyers were to be filled out with the names and addresses of our family and friends for the purpose of emotional extortion of money. My child was supposed to write a sob story about their dreams on one portion of this flyer. The flyers had to be turned in to the coach to be mailed; this way the coach and organization in charge of this sport could verify that all players had indeed completed the emotional-extortion flyers. This is wrong on so many levels. I do not in any way, shape, or form agree with using emotion and guilt to get people to send money. Leave that to the television evangelists. My tax dollars should be purchasing the uniforms the players need and the transportation needed to get them from game to game. The spending is out of control. There is no reason that people without much money should be struggling to give money for a school activity that we've already paid for through taxes!

My youngest daughter signed up for girls scouts. At the very first meeting we received a stack of fundraiser information. I notified the scout leaders that I don't participate in fundraisers; I pay for my children's activities myself. I asked how much the waiver fee was to *not* participate—some organizations have installed a waiver fee system for people like me who don't beg money from family, friends and neighbors, which I like—I was told that there is no waiver fee to avoid participation and that by not participating it would hurt my daughter because she would not receive the participation badge. At the awards ceremony all the other girls would be receiving the badge for participating and completing the fundraiser, but my daughter would be left out. Once again…you've got to be kidding. More emotional extortion. Participate and go-with-the-flow or your child will be left out and ostracized. Personally, I don't feel that earning a badge for extorting money out of your family and friends is a badge I would be proud to sew on my daughters' sash or a trait that I want my children to become proficient at.

I have a budget, the school system has a budget, the government has a budget. Why can't anyone just say no. If something is outside the budget…just say no. Stop making every single thing in life about money! Stop forcing our children to be little emotional extortionists. Stop teaching them that in order to get what they want they better be really good little salespeople and know how to milk money from the people they care about.

I want to make a distinction between the non-necessary fundraising I am stating my case about and the fundraising that is actually necessary. For example, if someone has had a serious health issue and the ridiculousness of health care costs in this country have devastated them, I would be the first in line to give them money. That is fundraising for a purpose. Giving to help a fellow human being is a part of life that can make you feel really good inside; giving because you are made to feel guilty by somebody who thinks your kids need better sports uniforms than the kids in the next town is ridiculous.

*"Successful guilt is the bane of society."*
*—Publilius Syrus*

*"Debt is the slavery of the free."*
*—Publilius Syrus*

# No Accent over the e’

This is just a small topic but one I feel has worldwide interest.

Our planet is made up of many, many different languages and even among those speaking the same language there are many different accents.

I have made the discovery that I am one of the few who speak the English language with no accent at all. I can’t say if I would have an accent in any other language as I can’t speak any other language. That year of Spanish in high school was a waste of time. All I retained from that time was a t-shirt that says “te quero” (and I am not sure I can even spell it right) which means “I love you.”

I made this astounding “no accent” discovery while sitting in my car at a red light belting out a Toby Keith song. I have heard interviews with Toby Keith and heard the distinct southern drawl that he speaks with. But…and here is the kicker…when he sings he pronounces words just like I do! My heart thumped and my spirit soared when I realized that I was the one…that person that had NO accent at ALL!

After this initial discovery I was extremely excited, but still a little skeptical and felt that further research was needed. I spent the next several minutes continuing to listen to the radio and belting out song after song to see if it could really be possible. Olivia Newton-John is Australian and I have heard her speak during the enumerable times I have watched the movie *Grease*. She speaks with an accent, but during her song “Hopelessly Devoted to You” she pronounces her words just like I do. Wow…this is amazing.

On a not-so-interesting side note: I absolutely love the movie Grease. It is one of my favorites and I know EVERY song by heart. To show that I do have a little depth, another one of my favorite movies is *Gone With the Wind*, but I usually don’t have enough time to watch it all at one time. That’s a very…very…long…movie.

Next, came my collaboration with Elton John. He is British…I think…I can be very observant or thick as molasses depending on the given day. Anyway, Elton and I were "Crocodile Rockin'" and once again he sang his words exactly like I did. No accent. He and I were one. Given the ever expanding pile of evidence, I think it is very obvious that I truly have no accent. I plan to continue my research by collaborating with other artists like the Bee Gees, Mick Jagger, and Shania Twain, but until someone disproves my theory and indisputable evidence is provided, I will continue to believe that I have no accent.

FYI – I am from a small town in Pennsylvania called Mount Joy. It is a quiet, little town in Lancaster County and thought you might want to visit to see if it is only me or if others from my area have managed to attain this same specialness.

*"A true friend is someone who thinks that you are a good egg even though he knows that you are slightly cracked."*
*—Bernard Meltzer*

# Don't Call Me Ma'm

I am sure there are several topics in this book that will raise the hackles of many. This one will be no exception.

Politically incorrect terminology drives me crazy. By no means am I promoting that people run around being rude to their fellow human beings, but give me a break on the constant bombardment of terms that are now considered taboo.

When I first began hearing the cashiers at my local grocery store referring to me as ma'm, I knew I had reached middle age. I hate when they call me ma'm. It makes me feel old and necessitates facing the prospect that I am actually getting older.

You can call me girl. I AM a girl. On the day I was born my parents anxiously awaited the arrival of their third child because they already had two boys. They had decided to try one more time for a girl to make their family complete. My mother is very feminine and was ready to buy pink, curl some hair, and attach some ribbons. The doctor assists me as I slide into the world and he announces "It's a girl." So, bottom line is…I am a girl. You can call me girl until I am ninety years old and peeing my pants as I sip my dinner through a straw. You can call me a drunk because I am Irish, you can call me weak because I am a woman, you can call me cracker because I am white; I just don't care. If some arrogant gentleman decides someday to use the term girl in a derogatory manner I will simply smile and walk away knowing that I could run rings around him in a battle of wit and it is only his need to lessen my worth to enhance his own feelings of inadequacy that produced the word "girl" from his lips. The only way he gains any power over me by speaking in that manner is if I give it credence by reacting angrily. Just like a bully in school…the only way you give them power is if you react. A bully thrives in gaining power through making others feel inadequate. Don't react…take their power… and they deflate.

We cannot control the actions of any other human being. We can only control ourselves. Trying to make the entire population use all the politically correct terminology is just annoying. Quit trying to control what everyone else is saying and doing and focus on yourself. Quit blaming everyone else for the current circumstances in your life and decide to take responsibility for your own life. Realize that whatever is happening in your life and whatever road your life is taking…you are responsible. When reaching the end of a bad marriage don't look at your partner and say "it's all your fault." It's not. It can't be. You were BOTH there and don't forget that YOU married him or her. Your previous decision brought you to where you are. I am so tired of hearing people whine about who is at fault for their present state of affairs.

Sticks and stones can break my bones but names will never hurt me, so, you can call me girl (just don't hit me with a rock or call me ma'm) because that is what I am…a girl and in control of my life. No matter what you call me, it does not affect how I feel about myself. I am what I am and I like what I am.

*"God helps those who help themselves."*
*—Benjamin Franklin*

# Retain Your Immaturity

I have been known to say that I will never grow up and maturity is not something I strive for. I mean what I say. Maturity is totally overrated. I think you can be responsible without being mature.

I arrive home from work with aching feet and need the solace of my big, cushy, leopard-printed, fuzzy slippers. I slide my feet out of the work shoes and can practically hear their sigh of relief as the odor vapors waft up past my knees and my toes spread themselves out in rapturous freedom.

After the glorious release of foot from shoe, I search out my slippers and with great relish slip my feet into their warmth and comfort; just about that time one of my children will announce that they need a notebook for school tomorrow, cupcakes for the holiday party, or a ride to school for an unannounced extra practice. I used to look sadly at my feet, slip off the slippers and slide back into the shoes with a groan of misery from my feet.

As I have aged, my maturity level has actually dropped. I am becoming one of those old people that will fart on a metal chair and laugh about it, wear my fuzzy slippers to the school or grocery store, or sit at a soccer game in my "loungewear" which is just a fancy name for pajama pants. My need to worry about what the neighbors will think is waning with each passing day and I think many of them secretly envy me.

I recall a day when I had had enough of an old computer desk that was literally falling apart at the seams. I had tried unsuccessfully to sell it at garage sales and tried to dispose of it through the trash pick-up. If I had been mature I would have found an adult way of disposing of the desk, instead my immaturity took the helm and I wrestled the desk into the front yard, marched back into my garage to retrieve a sledgehammer and spent the next half hour expelling loud karate-like grunts as I swung the rather large sledgehammer at the desk splintering it into a million pieces. Damn, that felt good.

I was so enraptured in my cathartic desk-destroying that I hadn't even realized that most of the people in my small, six-house cul-de-sac were out in front of their houses pointing and laughing. What would they all do for entertainment if I were mature too?

Another area that is a worry for me are the other adults in my children's lives who have forgotten their inner child; the instructors, coaches, teachers, and school administrators that have crawled and fought their way out of childhood and forgotten the way back.

One particular school official comes to mind when I am thinking of this topic. He was in charge of keeping the peace among the students and disciplinary action when needed. This gentleman took his job a little too seriously. I think he forgot to examine his motives and retain his immaturity. He was far too serious and treated the students and school like a military outpost. Needless to say he was very unpopular with students and parents alike.

A few years after his hiring and subsequent torture of the students, he was abruptly fired for having sex with the school secretary in the principal's office (Actually, I think he and the secretary resigned, at least that's what the paper said). Although the principal is supposed to be "a prince and a pal" (get it? Princ-i-pal) the school's principal was not amused.

Now my problem with this situation is that this school official expected perfection out of his students, left no room for laughing, hugging a friend, tossing a little bit of pudding now and again, YET, he did not expect quite as much perfection out of himself or his secretary. No wonder so many kids are on antidepressants. The impossible and completely unattainable perfection expected of kids packs them firmly into a pressure cooker that will eventually explode. These adults need to examine their motives. I believe this particular instance is one of a need for power. This school official had some situation as a child that made him feel powerless and he now had all the power he could possibly want and used it or was just an arrogant, power-hungry jerk. If he had examined his motives he may have seen this and taken a short trip back through the tunnel to childhood to retrieve his lost immaturity. He needed to go back and find his inner child.

I am reminded of a particularly interesting moment during my early parenting years. I had three children at that time: one six-year-old son, one three-year-old son and a year old baby daughter. I had been working a long time…a very long time…on potty training both my boys. I had actually been working on potty training my oldest son for going on two years…sheesh. He simply didn't want to do it. He didn't care what everyone else was doing in preschool those days…he just was NOT going to do it…I am digressing again. I thought the training of my younger son would help my older son so I tried to make potty-time fun and full of togetherness for the two. I had sent the two boys to the bathroom together to try to "tinkle" before we left the house. They were in there what seemed like an exceptionally long time and giggling could be heard…never a good sign. I walked into the bathroom to see little penises flailing and pee streams headed in every direction. "WHAT are you boys doing?" I asked. They looked up at me with a look of surprise and confusion. They were totally immersed in their fantasy world. Apparently they were pretending they were Darth Vader and Luke Skywalker. They were using their penis's as light sabers and crossing the streams. The result was about three drops of little-boy-pee in the toilet and the rest was running down walls and puddling on the floor.

The school administrator that was so tough on his students needed to try and find his light saber and not for use on Princess Lay-me…oops, I mean Leia.

*"Youth is a circumstance you can't do anything about.*
*The trick is to grow up without getting old."*
*—Frank Lloyd Wright*

*"Never make the same mistake twice or you'll never get around*
*to all of them."*
*—Unknown Author*

# The Holiday Conspiracy

Another bit of proof to my theory that we human beings are suffering from lemming-syndrome is the adhering to holiday traditions no matter how *nuts* those holiday traditions are.

Long, long ago events occurred that brought about the urge to remember or relive those moments. I just don't happen to believe that the baloney holidays we celebrate today bear that much resemblance to those original events.

How did Jesus Christs' birth become a day to run around giving presents to family members, mailman, school teacher, paperboy, neighbor, and every other person you come across? How did this original event morph into a day jumbled with food, family, a guy in a red suit, cookie baking, neon reindeer, snowmen in the front yard, and houses plastered with multi-colored lights?

I especially don't understand the cookie baking. This could be because I do not particularly enjoy cooking or baking. It just seems to be so much work for the end product. The grocery store bakery makes great chocolate-chip cookies so why would I want to spend days covered in flour, splattering my kitchen walls—and everything else within ten feet of the mixer—with batter? I hear so many women lamenting the coming of the Christmas season because it means they have to begin the month-long ritual of baking every kind of cookie known to man and then running from house to house providing plates of said cookies. The weird part is other women are doing the same and bringing their baked goods to *your* house. All you really did was spend a month exhausting yourself baking cookies for everyone else only to have them do the exact same thing for you. Maybe the tradition should change to everyone taking the month of December off…*buying* a couple dozen cookies…and then sitting down to chat with friends while sending some birthday wishes and respect the way of Jesus.

As for the gift-giving, my philosophy on that subject is do away with it. Get together and think about all you have and how fortunate you are to be walking and breathing on this beautiful planet. Gift-giving has become a chore done in the name of a famous historical figure. Really?…I think the advertising industry has perpetuated all this craziness and we need to "just say no!" I often wonder what Jesus would say if he could sit through one of our Christmas seasons. He would probably be shaking his head saying "what in the hell are you people thinking!".

Easter is another holiday I just don't get. Good Friday seems to be working…most people who honor this holiday go to a service or remembrance of some type on the day Jesus died. Then you get to Easter Sunday; parents fill baskets with chocolate bunnies, colorful plastic grass and probably toys…then hide the aforementioned baskets for the children to find in the morning. What!? Jesus is more than likely thinking what silly creatures we are for hiding chocolate rabbits in remembrance of the day he arose from the dead.

Thanksgiving is the one holiday I don't have much of a problem with. It has developed into a pretty darn gratifying day of celebration. I happen to love my family, eating, and football, so Thanksgiving is my favorite. Sitting around a table saying how thankful I am for my wonderful family, eating until I roll from the table like a one-hundred-forty-pound bowling ball, then plopping down on a comfy couch to fritter away the afternoon hanging with the important people in my life and watching football sounds really enjoyable to me. Luckily, most of the important people in my life are great cooks; not much for me to do but enjoy it. Yeee-haaa!

As for most of the other eight million holidays we have per year, I blame it all on the greeting card companies, advertisers and the retail contingency. I am a firm believer in treating people the way I want to be treated. I prefer to use human decency on a daily basis, then try to make up for it on Valentine's Day, Mother's Day, Father's Day, Grandparents's Day, Boss's Day, Secretary's Day…I dug out my calendar and there are twenty-three holidays/observances listed on it. The best holidays are the ones that give you a paid day off, but with no family, gift-giving, or card-giving obligations. Stop the madness! No more senseless holidays. No more allowing the greeting card companies to get rich playing on our guilt. Don't allow these "cardboard tycoons" to drive you to the greeting card aisle one more time to purchase their million-dollar pieces of thick paper. Wake up to the conspiracy that is all around you. The greeting card companies, the retail stores and their minions (the advertisers) are all getting rich while we are throwing our money away on pieces of cardboard that most people read and throw away. Save yourself the trouble and just take your money directly to the trash can and insert. Wasn't that much easier? And the best part is you didn't have to use ten dollars worth of gas running to the supermarket or drug store to throw your money away and the recipient of the card doesn't have to receive a nasty paper cut on the envelope trying to open it. Everybody wins!

*"Christmas is the season when you buy this year's gifts with next year's money."*
*—Unknown Author*

# Too Many Moving Parts

This is likely to be another one of the more unpopular topics. After many years of hormonal soul searching I have come to the conclusion that we women really are nuts, but it is most definitely not our fault.

I own two lawn mowers. One of my mowers is the old-fashioned reel mower which consists of a handle, two wheels and a spinning blade. When you push the reel mower the blade turns and it cuts the grass. When you stop pushing the reel mower it stops cutting the grass. This is a fairly simple piece of machinery to use. The only drawback to the reel mower is that is can't cut the grass within about 12 inches of my flower beds that contain mulch. The wood mulch pieces cause the blade to get stuck. Very annoying. My second mower is a mulching push mower. In order to use this mower you have to go to the gas station and fill a little container with fuel, bring that fuel home and pour it into the mower, check the oil tank, move the throttle, grasp the pull cord and yank until you've thrown out your back and neck to get it started, then push it and it cuts the grass. I have kept the mulching mower because it can cut the grass in the annoying one foot area surrounding my flowerbeds that may contain a few pieces of mulch. The mulching mower just chops it up or spits it directly out and keeps on going.

The two mowers have their benefits and their drawbacks and each has a specific job to do in my yard. Men are the reel mower and we women are the mulching mower. We do basically the same things. We go through life walking, talking, working, searching for meaningful relationships, and ultimately some of us procreate.

Men's bodies are the less complicated models that all you have to do is push. Women's bodies take much more maintenance and therefore we have quite a few more things that can go wrong. We women have a few different parts that require oiling, lubricating, and cajoling to get them to function.

The additional parts and hormones wreak havoc with us and this is by none of our own doing. So, the next time you say a woman is bonkers…you are probably right…but, remember there is not a darn thing she can do about all the parts and maintenance it takes to keep her running.

Think about orgasms. If you touch a man's penis he will orgasm. I heard a comedienne one time describe making a woman orgasm is as complicated as a Nintendo cheat code. You need to talk to a woman and seduce her brain, you need to hold hands with a woman to seduce her emotions, you need to help her with the housework and children to seduce her sense of responsibility, and finally if you get anywhere near her genitalia, you need to gently coerce many different parts into action and when you have finally accomplished all of that she *may* have an orgasm. And then again she may not.

So just remember that like that video game you enjoy so much…it may require the conquering of many levels to reach the pinnacle of the game, but the sense of accomplishment can be a wonderful feeling. If, however, you feel the end result is not worth the work…get a dog.

*"Women need a reason to have sex. Men just need a place."*
*—Billy Crystal*

*"Women might be able to fake orgasms, but men can fake whole relationships."*
*—Sharon Stone*

# Gemini?

For many years now I have tried to decide whether I am a social butterfly or an anti-social grizzly bear. I have moments when I enjoy people and interacting with them and I have other times when, if my doorbell or phone rings, my eyes roll up in my head and I drop to the floor in a fetal position at the prospect of interacting with someone.

I am a Gemini. I am not sure if I put a whole lot of stock in the birth signs being able to tell a lot about a person, but one does have to wonder. Gemini is the sign of the twin. I totally relate to that Alanis Morissette song that goes something like "I'm a bitch, I'm a lover, I'm a child, I'm a mother, I'm a sinner, I'm a saint, I do not feel ashamed." I can be a total lazy-ass one day and a workaholic the next, swear like a sailor today and be Mary Sunshine tomorrow. It just doesn't make much sense. Who am I really? I guess it's possible that human beings can have chameleon-like abilities also.

I have come to the conclusion that anyone who would like to see me on a social basis has to sneak up on me. When a spontaneous visit with someone has arisen, I generally have a wonderful time and go home smiling and talking about how I need to get together with that person on a more regular basis. Two weeks later that same person can decide on a whim to stop and visit me for a few minutes and I want to lock myself in the bathroom.

There was absolutely no reason for including this other than just saying it out loud; an admission of one of my many quirky traits. I believe in admitting all of my faults up front; that way no one can accuse me of anything I haven't already warned them about. If they continue to speak to me, then they do it at their own risk.

There are a few exceptions to my basic tendencies. I never have a time when I don't enjoy being with my children. They are just too fun. My significant other is also an exception. He knows me so well that I don't have to be or do anything. We can just be in the same room with no communication and enjoy each other's company. He makes me feel at ease. And the last exception is my best friend. She and I have been friends for over twenty years and, like my significant other, she knows everything there is to know. She has seen all the warts and keeps hanging around anyway. She keeps me out of trouble and I help get her into some.

I thought it might be fun to list some of the more famous Gemini's. Quite an eclectic group: Alanis Morissette, Angelina Jolie, Tim Allen, Anne Heche, Bob Dylan, Bob Hope, Boy George, Marilyn Monroe, Judy Garland, Lenny Kravitz, Frank Lloyd Wright, Joan Collins, Joan Rivers, Johnny Depp, Donald Trump, Clint Eastwood, Brooke Shields, Michael J. Fox, Mike Myers, Paul McCartney, Ralph Waldo Emerson, John F. Kennedy, and Venus Williams.

*"I have a gay side to me and also a sad side.*
*That's a real problem."*
*—Marilyn Monroe*

# Things No One Should Ever Do

1. Never do Elvis impersonations in the white sequined Jumpsuit. Other imitations are perfectly fine. I love Elvis, but even he should not have worn the white sequined jumpsuits.
2. Never spit on your hand and clean your child's face. It's just gross. I do it.
3. Never wear a comb-over on a windy day or any day. We have all seen them. The gentleman who is losing his hair on top and allows one side to grow reeeeaaaallly long and then comb's it from one side over the top to the other side. Then said gentleman goes out on a windy day and the comb over loses its grip on the opposite side of the head and begins flapping out one side like a neon sign blinking "Look! I do comb-overs!". It is just sad when a man can't admit he is losing hair in some spots. Just face it. I have seen many sexy men who have decided to just shave the errant hair off and they are sexy for two reasons: One because they are confident enough to face the aging process with grace and two because bald can be very sexy when done right.
4. Never piss off Naomi Campbell.
5. Never marry a man who asks you to wax his back. Really you shouldn't marry a woman who asks you to wax her back either. This is good advice either way.
6. Never use too many words that begin with the letter "P" in one sentence. It causes you to spit on the other participant in the conversation. This can be very awkward once it happens. Do you ignore the fact that you just sent a huge spit wad flying toward the other person or do you just go ahead and speak about the "big, pink elephant" in the middle of the room; namely your spit.
7. Never wear Erkel pants. Steve Erkel was that adorable

kid on the television show "Family Matters." He wore the waistband of his pants up somewhere in the rib area. I have actually seen people that do that in real life. First of all, it can't be comfortable and second, if you have that much trouble keeping your pants up that they need to start in the rib area…move to a nudist colony.

8. Never wear bowling shoes.
9. Never french Kiss in a slobbery manner. French kissing should be a slow, soft, dry, event. Lips should softly touch with tongues joining here and there, subtley moving and tantalizing. Opening your mouth like a snake unhinging its jaws to swallow a mouse is never necessary! And your tongue should at no point tickle the tonsils of your partner. Yuk.
10. Never make fun of Cher. She rocks!
11. Never tattoo the likeness or name of any one on your body. The only possible exception to the tattoo rule would be the name or face of one of your children, but even that is risky considering when you are ninety they may stuff you into a nursing home where you get nothing to eat except applesauce and then never come to visit.
12. Never watch Martha Stewart. It raises the bar too high. I think she's a robot.
13. Never participate in cup-stacking as a sport. I think this is self-explanatory. I will be highly disappointed if I see this on the Olympic schedule next time around.
14. Never wear shoes or bras. This alone could make half the population of the United States less edgy.
15. Never choose a spouse while intoxicated. Enough said.
16. Never send money to a television evangelist. They already have God's blessing; what more do they need? Jim and Tammy Faye. Need I say more?
17. Never ask Larry the Cable Guy to model a speedo. No one should model a speedo unless his name is "Longhorn" and he is wearing nothing but a cowhide speedo, chaps and dancing at your sister's bachelorette party.
18. Never pick your nose while sitting in your car at a traffic light. And if you really need to, don't inspect the results.

# The End

I hope you have enjoyed, have laughed, been stimulated, been irritated and your brain is swimming with all of the great party conversations in this book. I am not right, I am not wrong. I am not an expert on anything, but know just enough about many areas to be dangerous.

I am just someone with lots of thoughts and I can be persuaded—with good argument—to change my thinking on any topic. I love a good debate and I love intelligence. There is nothing better in life than a fantastically stimulating conversation with an extremely intelligent, yet reasonable fellow human being. I really enjoy being given a new thought or idea to give my brain a workout. Close-mindedness is a curse; don't give in to it.

We are born and from the first second begin learning. To me, learning is what life is all about. I would like to go to school forever. I would go to learn more about the law, how the body works and psychology. Psychology is of particular interest because figuring out what makes people tick is fascinating. I also have a great amount of interest in nature and a master gardening course would be fun. Nature has so many answers that we have just wandered away from.

Thus far in life I have worked as a computer operator for a bank, I ran the office of an amazingly creative woman who did religious talks through flowers, I worked as the receptionist and bookkeeper for a hair salon, I have been a church secretary, I went to school to get a real estate license and I have taken cake decorating classes. Each job has come about because I was trying to work my way around raising my children without dealing with childcare. I thought I was just doing each of these jobs to make ends meet while placing my priority on raising my children. Each of these jobs have allowed me to spend more time being a mom, but they have also been amazing experiences. I have learned something from each and every one. I have met incredible people and have a plethora of fabulous memories to go with each experience. I was an art major in high school, but was also really drawn to the possibility of working as a nurse in the health care industry. I now operate a cleaning business, code manuscripts at night and throughout my adult years have written and illustrated books for my children (not published and professional, just stories about them for fun). I particularly enjoy coding the manuscripts. It is like Christmas each time I pick up my work because I have no idea what type of book will be in the envelope. Will I be learning something about politics, religion, cooking, psychology, or just typing a mystery novel. Being a mom is the best job that I have had and also the most enlightening. I have learned more by being a mother than from any other area of life.

I joke a lot about my old boyfriends and my ex-husband, but really I have no regrets. Each person comes into your life for a reason and you need to stop and think about the lessons you learn from each situation. If you contemplate all of the good and bad experiences in your life you will realize that without the bad experiences your road to wisdom would be stunted. A life full of nothing but ease leaves you with not much life experience and some very "vanilla" stories to tell in your old age. A life full of trials and tribulations— in essence a life full of hard knocks—will make you a stronger and wiser person with colorful stories to tell your cronies in the old folks home. With great pain comes great growth.

I still don't know what I want to be when I grow up, so I have decided to not grow up. When the time comes that I am no longer curious and feel I have learned all I want to know, I imagine it will be time to bring the curtain down.

*"Aim for success, not perfection. Never give up your right to be wrong, because then you will lose the ability to learn new things and move forward with your life."*
*—Dr. David M. Burns*

*"If people around you aren't going anywhere, if their dreams are no bigger than hanging out on the corner, or if they're dragging you down, get rid of them. Negative people can sap your energy so fast, and they can take your dreams from you, too."*
*—Earvin Johnson*

# About the Author

Average American, forty-something, single mother of four, works too much, terrible health insurance, struggling financially, out of shape, car breaks down every month, and HAPPY AS A LARK!